KW-254-783

Boys Don't Cry

BOYS AND SEXISM IN EDUCATION

Sue Askew and Carol Ross

Cover and text illustrations by Carol Ross

Open University Press
Milton Keynes · Philadelphia

Open University Press
Celtic Court
22 Ballmoor
Buckingham MK18 1XW

and
1900 Frost Road, Suite 101,
Bristol, PA 19007, USA

First Published 1988
Reprinted 1989, 1990, 1993

Copyright © 1988 Sue Askew and Carol Ross

All rights reserved. No part of this work may be reproduced
in any form by mimeograph or by any other means, without
permission in writing from the publisher.

British Library Cataloguing in Publication Data

Askew, Sue
  Boys don't cry : sexism in boys education. — (Gender
  and education).
  1. Sex discrimination in education —
  Great Britain   2. Sexism — Great Britain
  I. Title   II. Ross, Carol   III. Series
  370.19′345   LC212.83.G7
  ISBN 0-335-10296-4

Library of Congress Cataloging in Publication Data

Askew, Sue
  Boys don't cry: sexism in boys education
  Bibliography : p.
  Includes index
  1. Sex discrimination in education
  Great Britain   2. Sexism — Great Britain
I. Ross, Carol   II. Title
Library of Congress card Number 87-30158
ISBN 0-335-10296-4

Typeset by Burns & Smith, Derby
Printed in Great Britain by St Edmundsbury Press Ltd,
Bury St Edmunds, Suffolk

DMU 0362481 01 5

14712

310.19345/ASK

Boys Don't Cry

OPEN UNIVERSITY PRESS
Gender and Education Series
Editors
ROSEMARY DEEM
Professor of Educational Research, University of Lancaster
GABY WEINER
Professor of Education at South Bank University
TITLES IN THE SERIES

Managing Women
Sue Adler, Jenny Laney and Mary Packer

Boys Don't Cry
Sue Askew and Carol Ross

Science and Technology in the Early Years
Naima Browne (ed.)

Untying the Apron Strings
Naima Browne and Pauline France (eds)

Changing Perspectives on Gender
Helen Burchell and Val Millman (eds)

Co-education Reconsidered
Rosemary Deem (ed.)

Girls and Sexuality
Lesley Holly (ed.)

Women in Educational Management
Jenny Ozga

A History of Women's Education in England
June Purvis

Shaping Up to Womanhood
Sheila Scraton

'Race', Gender and the Education of Teachers
Iram Siraj-Blatchford (ed.)

Whatever Happens to Little Women?
Christine Skelton (ed.)

Dolls and Dungarees
Eva Tutchell (ed.)

Just a Bunch of Girls
Gaby Weiner (ed.)

Women and Training
Ann Wickham

DE MONTFORT UNIVERSITY
LIBRARY

Date 8/11/95

Loc./Form Risehdlme

Class 370.19345

Suffix ASK

Contents

Series Editor's Introduction

Over the past ten years, there has been a variety of publications on issues of gender and education, whether concerned with equal opportunities, anti-sexism, 'girl-friendly' or feminist approaches. In the main these have been publications, some in this series, which have sought to explain, challenge and/or change the position of girls and women in the education system, by deliberately focusing on female educational experiences, as teachers or pupils.

Concern for the needs of boys has been less of an issue because, it is argued, boys appear to receive more attention in 'mainstream' education, though it is also recognised that if the position of girls and women is to improve in education and in society, that of boys and men will have to change too.

This book, the fifth in the *Gender and Education* series, seeks to correct this omission by focusing specifically on boys, but does so from an anti-sexist perspective. It considers how masculinity is constructed in society and reinforced in schools, structurally and in everyday interaction. It refers to the schooling experiences of boys, whether taught in mixed or single-sex schools, and what impact they have on their teachers, particularly if they are women.

And finally, *Boys Don't Cry* provides a whole range of strategies and ideas which have been tried out and tested in schools by the authors in their development of an anti-sexist approach to the schooling of boys. Written in an accessible and lively style, this book will be of interest not only to teachers and researchers working with boys or concerned with reducing sex inequalities in education, but to parents and to the boys themselves.

Gaby Weiner

Introduction

Over the last five years we have been concerned with anti-sexism and education, particularly in relation to boys. For the first two of these years we worked at a secondary boys' school in East London, developing, monitoring and teaching a new anti-sexist course to all first- and second-year boys. Subsequently, we supported anti-sexist initiatives in the Inner London Education Authority (ILEA) boys' schools (including offering support to women teachers) and were involved in developing and making materials for anti-sexist curricular work with boys, working with boys-only groups in mixed schools, as well as in boys' schools. During this time we have visited schools (observing and participating in classrooms, attending meetings of Equal Opportunity Working Parties and Women's Groups, talking to teachers and running workshops); organised and led courses and workshops for teachers throughout ILEA; been invited to organise discussion on anti-sexist work with boys at Equal Opportunity conferences both within and outside ILEA; and discussed this work with teachers and parents throughout Britain.

We have worked in approximately thirty boys' schools and twenty mixed schools in all parts of London. Some of these schools were multi-cultural and multi-racial, some were predominantly white; some were in economically deprived areas and some in 'well-off' areas; some were Church schools. We have also worked in a range of primary schools throughout London. The issues we write about have emerged from these experiences.

This book is primarily about sexism in boys' schools. However, in writing about sexism in boys' schools we explore many issues which apply to all schools, including primary and further education establishments. We look at some of the ways in which boys are socialised; boys' behaviour at school both in the classroom and playground; and the effects of boys' behaviour both on each other and on other people. We explore the school structure as a social institution: the values and attitudes inherent in the organisation and structure of boys' schools; the social divisions built into the system; its underlying definitions of 'masculinity' in relation to 'femininity'. We look at the experiences of women teachers in relation to both the boys they teach and the institutions within which they work. We explore the implications of doing anti-sexist work with boys and with school staff, and look at some concrete strategies for both.

While we have not talked explicitly about gay boys and how they fare in school, we do look in detail at the construction of different masculinities and implicit in this are issues concerning notions of male sexuality. Our work also has implications for issues of heterosexism and is an expression of the homophobia inherent in 'norms' of maleness.

We feel that because of the range of social issues touched on in the book, it will be of interest not only to students and teachers in all phases of education, but also to parents and anyone working with boys, for example, in youth clubs and social work. Furthermore, the socialisation, behaviour and education of boys have implications for girls, and so the book has relevance for people concerned with the education of girls. We believe that sexism in schools is a microcosm of sexism in society. But we feel that sexism in boys' schools is particularly overt. Because it is a more polarised situation it can be easier to recognise how boys' schools operate as sexist institutions. We feel, therefore, that an understanding of sexism in boys' schools can illuminate how it is built into all schools.

We wanted to write this book because we think we have found some gaps in the literature of sexism and education. For example, not very much has been written about women teachers, beyond looking at their position in the school hierarchy; boys have been mainly written about only in so far as their behaviour affects girls. Their behaviour has not been sufficiently looked at in the context of why it occurs and how it is reinforced and perpetuated by the school system itself. We also felt that there has been a lot of interesting research relating to sexism in education which we wanted to draw together in the light of our experience in boys' schools.

Our initial involvement with anti-sexist work with boys did not come from any special commitment to working with boys only. On the contrary, as feminist teachers, we were more concerned with anti-sexist work with girls. However because of our particular employment circumstances we found ourselves working in a boys' school. This put us in a unique position over the last five years which has allowed us to explore the sorts of issue we raise in this book. As a result of this work, we have attempted to confront and examine why many of the approaches we took did not work as well as we had hoped. We were forced to consider a variety of issues surrounding what happens in the classroom. We realised that there were many layers and levels. Each time we identified a particular factor we became aware of other underlying features: dynamics within the classroom; relationships between the pupils; relationships between pupils and teachers; the school structure beyond the classroom; issues of racism and classism.

It may seem a contradiction to talk about addressing sexism in boys' schools. However, boyhood is the induction period into manhood . Boys themselves are victims of their socialisation and experience difficulties from the pressures they are put under to prove their masculinity and hide their vulnerability. As adult men it is true in one sense to say that they are still victims of their socialisation, but they are also perpetuators of sexism, and in a position of power (in a class-related way) over women.

It is not our intention in this book to identify boys as 'the problem': rather our aim is to locate boys' behaviour within the context of the social structure. We feel strongly that unless the social structure itself changes the power relationships between people in terms of race, class and gender will not change. Rehana Minhas (1986) writes:

> If racism and sexism are defined in terms of a problem of individual attitudes and personal prejudices — often unintentional — then we cannot begin to deal effectively with the

varying manifestations of these inequalities. Attitudes and ideas, moreover, do not exist in a vacuum but are rooted in the economic/political/legal and social system.

We believe that anti-sexist work with girls is very important, for example, changes in the organisation and content of certain subjects to allow girls to succeed in male-dominated areas of the curriculum, such as maths and science. It is also important to examine the things that may be negatively affecting girls' education, such as the amount and kind of teacher attention they get in mixed classrooms. But we also feel that the position of girls will not really change fundamentally until the underlying nature of the school as an institution changes.

However, the curriculum is the level which is most accessible for teachers to change. Within the curriculum there are different approaches to equal opportunity work. One is at an explicit level which involves teaching children to be aware of and to negotiate sexism (for example, assertiveness training and self-defence for girls). At an implicit level we can work towards reorganising the way a given school subject itself is constructed as a body of knowledge, the language of the subject, the content and the teaching methodology. The limitation of explicit anti-sexist work is that it puts the onus for changing sexism on the pupils themselves — when actually they are not in a position of power to change the system. The explicit approach may be useful at a personal, individual level, but it is not going to change the ways sexism is structured in an institution. It can affect self-image and confidence, and this may mean that when pupils are adults they will want to fight to change the social system in which they live.

The aims of explicit anti-sexist work with boys and with girls are very different; for example, boys learning to be more co-operative and take on more caring roles; girls being encouraged to enter 'male'-dominated subjects and to be more assertive in their social interaction. However, anti-sexist aims relating to the reorganisation of subject areas apply equally to both girls and boys. This work involves making structural changes to the curriculum which would redress the balance of control by the dominant social group within subject disciplines. Baran (1986) describes the way we have to rethink the science curriculum at the more 'implicit' level:

Encouraging girls to pursue an interest and/or career in Science and Technology cannot be done by a few cosmetic and structural alterations ... It is very important to: challenge stereotypes; develop new images; demonstrate the relationship between interesting career prospects and the need for qualifications; consider the need for girl-only groups or introduce an element of compulsion at the option stage. However, these measures alone will make little impact, particularly in relationship to the majority of working class girls, unless we are prepared to re-think what Science education is, what it is for, and how we are going to teach it.

These are some of the issues we explore in the book. We write this book in the spirit of a 'discussion document' — these are our thoughts arising from our experiences of anti-sexist work with boys. We hope the reader will find it thought-provoking and a useful basis for taking these ideas further.

CHAPTER 1

The Construction of Masculinity

During the last two years we have talked to hundreds of teachers from over one hundred primary, secondary and special schools in one Local Education Authority. All of these teachers contacted us, or attended courses, because they are concerned about the 'problems' associated with boys[1] (Chapter 2 of this book describes these 'problems' in more detail). Such problems include domination in the mixed classroom by boys and boys' use of space, for example in the playground. These descriptions point to the need for girls' education to be reassessed with considerable urgency and many teachers want to work with boys as a way of trying to minimise the 'problems' and because they see much of boys' behaviour as having a detrimental effect on the boys' learning and on the boys themselves. They also see it as a direct outcome of inequalities in school and in wider society.

Talking about boys' behaviour can itself lead to reinforcing gender stereotypes: the number of boys who are a 'problem' might be fairly small in any one class. Not all boys are aggressive, demanding and disruptive. Those that are may be so for a variety of reasons. They may be reacting against inappropriate work; may need extra help in terms of developing particular skills, or may be reacting against a whole number of things in and outside the educational system itself. What is important is that, for whatever reason, it is boys rather than girls who are reacting in ways perceived to be a problem and receiving an unfair share of teacher attention, albeit some of it very negative.

A gender focus may help to explain some surprising and worrying facts. For example, the Fish Report (1985) on special needs showed that of all pupils in schools for emotionally disturbed behaviour 86.6 per cent are boys; boys have more problems learning to read.[2] In the old days of the 11 plus it was established that boys did worse than girls and so the pass mark for boys was lower than for girls. There is evidence to suggest that the grading of primary pupils in at least one Education Authority discriminates against girls in the same way (Toynbee 1985). Boys have been shown in recent research (Mahoney 1985) to make life exceedingly irksome, if not unpleasant, for girls. It is not uncommon to hear the comment: 'Boys mature later than girls'. Indeed, we remember thinking as adolescents in co-ed schools that the boys were childish and beneath our notice. But all this is 'common-sense' understanding. It is unproblematic for some people. Our contention is that it *is* problematic and that the way in which masculinity is constructed in our society might provide clarification on it. Our 'common-sense' understandings and the significance we give to particular things themselves arise out of a particular political and social situation. We may not realise the theoretical significance or importance of what has happened to us.

What are the stereotypes of boys/men?

This chapter focuses on how boys learn to be male. How do boys get a sense of themselves as male from which their masculinity is constructed? Boys learn the kind of behaviour by which they can express their masculinity. It seems likely that many different factors contribute to this sense of 'maleness', but here we discuss those aspects which seem to have direct implications for learning and behaviour at school.

There is a *dominant* view of men with which we are bombarded through the press and other media. This view of men represents them as being tough, strong, aggressive, independent, brave, sexually active, rational, intelligent, and so on. The corresponding view of women is that they are vulnerable, weak, non-aggressive, kind, caring, passive, frightened, stupid, dependent and immature.[3] It is interesting that the descriptive words used for women are also those which are used for children.

Lloyd (1985) points out that this also creates a conflict for young men between being young, with all that implies, and being men, with all that implies. The contradiction, he suggests, is both confusing and complicated because all young men are affected by this dominant view of masculinity though mediated by their race and class position. While these stereotypes are obviously damaging and prevent young men from developing their full potential, they are also internalising extremely negative images of girls and women.

Trefor Lloyd writes that upper-middle-class men are expected to be aloof, to rule and to be separate from 'the others'. They are sent to boarding school at an early age, intimidated by older boys, and then offered the opportunity to do the same. It is also interesting to consider how they see women in the cut-off male world of the boarding school and to speculate on the fact that warmth, caring and empathy for others is severely curtailed by this practice of sending very young children away from their parents (see 'Private schools confront boys' hidden emotions', *Times Educational Supplement*, 18 April 1986). Lloyd argues that middle-class men are expected to be good with their brains, to be self-reliant, made to compete, told it is better to think than to do. Working-class images of masculinity, argues Lloyd, are perhaps most pervasive. They are seen as rough, tough, loud, beer-swilling, good at fighting, and more able to 'do' than to think. The idea that black and/or working-class men are more 'macho' and sexist than white middle-class men is another stereotype.

Value ascribed to stereotypical traits

Stereotypical traits are value-laden. Those which are assigned to the men who have power in our society are generally those which are seen as being desirable. A large sample of Americans was asked in the 1970s to list the characteristics, attributes and types of behaviour in which they thought men and women differed. Both men and women expressed a preference for the behaviour they had designated male. For example, traits described as follows were seen as *both* masculine and as desirable: very aggressive, very independent, not at all emotional, almost always hiding emotions, very objective, not at all easily influenced, very dominant, liking maths and science very much, very active, very competitive, very logical, never crying, very ambitious, talking freely with other men about sex, thinking men are always superior to women, and very active. Traits opposed to these were all seen as feminine and less desirable. Out of the forty-one traits that the sample was asked to list, only twelve were seen as feminine *and* desirable. These were: doesn't use harsh language, very talkative, very tactful, very gentle, very aware of feelings of others, very neat in habits, very strong need for security, enjoys art and literature, and easily expresses tender feelings. While indicating that men and women *are* seen differently this study showed that masculine behaviour is *valued* more highly. The qualities ascribed to middle-class masculine behaviour are also those which are implicitly valued in Western society and in its major institutions. Schools are centrally places of 'reason', 'objectivity', 'competitiveness' and 'logic'. Boys and girls are expected to aspire to these ends if they are to 'succeed'.

There are still arguments about whether or not the types of stereotypical trait we have listed are based on observable differences between the sexes. We feel this is not true. Women as a whole are not passive, illogical, unselfconfident, just as men as a whole are not active, adventurous, ambitious and aggressive. Individual women and individual men vary greatly in their characteristics and behaviours. These traits are assigned to men and women by those who hold the dominant positions in society in order to secure and perpetuate the positions of privilege which result from a society based on inequality. Stereotyped traits are extremely dangerous both because they limit expectations and because we internalise the myths to a greater or lesser degree and either limit our own behaviour to fit in with them or else see ourselves as abnormal (of course, others will see us as abnormal as well!).

Apart from denying these stereotypes we are also concerned to challenge the value ascribed to traits considered to be 'masculine'. If young people are taught to be very competitive, to always act as leader, to be very independent and very ambitious, they are being offered a view of the world which reinforces ideas about winners and losers, some being powerful and others being powerless, some being strong and some being weak, some being equal and some inferior. It seems to us that a caring, humanitarian society is one based on equality, compassion, collaboration and interdependence.

Boys learning to be boys

We take it as given that much of the behaviour described as 'masculine' is learned (as opposed to being innate) and reinforced by stereotyped ideas about what it means to be male in this society. Baby boys and girls are treated very differently from birth. They are spoken to differently, dressed differently, played with differently, and there are different expectations for them. Nicholson (1984) writes:

> Take a baby out into the street, stop the first twenty people you meet ... ask them to hold 'Mark' and tell you what sort of baby he is. Repeat the procedure ... this time ask them what they think of 'Mary'. The baby will be the same in both cases ... Whatever the baby's real sex, 'Mark' will be described as bouncing, cheeky, mischievous and strong; while 'Mary' will be seen as lovely, sweet, gorgeous and cute.

An experiment at Sussex University (Smith and Lloyd 1978) invited thirty-two mothers to play with a baby they had never seen before and filmed the results. The same baby was presented to the mothers as either a 'boy' or a 'girl'. As you would guess the toys which the women chose for the baby were very different, depending on whether it was thought the baby was a girl or a boy: a doll for a girl, a hammer for a boy. But, more interestingly, they interpreted the same behaviour differently, depending on whether they thought it was a girl or a boy. When the baby became restless and they thought it was a boy, it was interpreted as a wish to play; so the women played with 'him'. When they thought it was a girl and she started to wriggle, the behaviour was interpreted as an indication that 'she' was upset and she was soothed.

It seems to us that if this is typical it is teaching boys and girls powerful messages about the way they manipulate and control their environment. Boys are being taught to demand attention and to control situations to get what they want; whereas girls are being taught to be passive and wait before reacting. If this is true, it has far-reaching consequences for adult behaviour.

The stereotype of 'active' male and 'passive' female can be applied to many situations: men are expected to be 'better at sport'; women are expected to assume supportive roles. If boys do learn to negotiate their environment more actively then this has enormous implications for learning, particularly for learning which involves experiment and investigation. We do not want to perpetuate any stereotypes about girls as passive recipients of knowledge, and boys as active 'makers' of knowledge, but to ask questions about how far socialisation of boys and girls affects the learning process.

Parents are clearly powerful role models for young children and it is still mothers who do most nurturing. Nicholson (1984) points to evidence which suggests that fathers tend to be more physical when playing (particularly so with boys). If so, that would fit in with a suggestion that boys and men do learn to value action rather than emotional closeness and communication in relationships. He also argues that there is evidence to suggest that men are more concerned than women that their sons should be 'masculine' and their daughters 'feminine'.

The books and other media images which children of all ages read still suggest very stereotyped roles. It seems to us that the majority of television programmes watched by our young children are showing male heroes in a variety of violent postures. Stories abound about baddies and goodies, with very little difference between them, except the goodies have 'right' on their side. Most cartoons for children are a variant of this theme and involve fairly horrific incidents. Recent Home Office research (see *The Sunday Times*, 15 December 1985) has shown that young children do, as parents have always known, copy the heroes they see on television. Female characters, if they are shown at all, are 'helped' out of trouble or stand around admiringly, or are just shown as plain stupid. Recently there have been one or two cartoons with central female characters (for example 'She Ra', 'He Man's' twin sister). These characters are all beautiful in a stereotyped way, but more muscular than usual, and they fight the baddies at their own game and win. Interestingly, one of us has noticed that the two four-year-old girls who live with her have suddenly taken to sword-fighting 'for the honour of Graysculls' (like She Ra) and to joining battle with their boy neighbours in a way which is quite new since these new heroines appeared. Advertisements for toys on television for young children are extremely stereotypical. Girls are always shown playing either with toys which copy adult 'women's' roles, such as toy cookers, toy hoovers, or tea sets, or they are shown with soft cuddly animals. Girls are even encouraged to buy 'My First Sink', and a 'head' on which they can practise putting make-up and putting in curlers. Boys, on the other hand, quite predictably are shown playing with games, cars, mechanical toys or space monsters. Most of these are now toys which are taken straight from the violent cartoons mentioned earlier, and the main aim of playing with the toy is to battle it out with an opponent.

Even when boys and girls are playing with the same toy it appears, from our personal observation, that they are often playing with it very differently. When a little girl plays with a doll she very often plays at being 'mother'. She feeds the doll, takes it for walks, bathes and dresses it. Boys, on the other hand, play very differently with action-man type dolls. They *are* the doll: taking part in an elaborate fantasy about fighting and killing. Girls' play revolves around relating to a second person (the doll); boys are the 'heroes' of their own play. One of us watched her daughter playing with cars. At last she thought she was observing a breakthrough, until she realised that her daughter was also playing 'mummies and daddies' with the cars — mummy car, daddy car and baby car!

Research has shown that an awareness of characteristics which are appropriate for each gender develops very early. Kuhn *et al.* (1978) presented two- to three-year-olds with two paper dolls, Michael and Lisa, and played a game where they asked about the characteristics and gender roles. At two years of age both boys and girls believed that girls would clean the house when they were grown up, and that boys would be the boss and mow the lawn.

The language we use to young children also reinforces the positions, expectations and 'stereotypes' of 'masculine' and 'feminine' behaviour in this society. Browne and France (1985) noted that in observations, tape and video recordings which they made of interactions between adults and children in nurseries that nicknames are gender-related.

> Girls were bombarded with terms of endearment — 'honey', 'sweetie', 'lovey', 'darling', 'treasure', 'precious', 'little charmer' … whereas boys got terms that reinforce the tough behaviour expected of them — 'buster', 'bruiser', 'toughie', 'big bully', 'wise guy', and so on … It is comforting for children to receive terms of endearment when they are sincerely meant. In our experience these terms are hardly ever offered to older boys in the nursery — for some reason it is 'unmanly' for them to be given signs of warmth and affection.

Before boys even leave the nursery stereotyped notions of masculinity are already absorbed.

Boys learning to be aggressive

One of the most worrying aspects which we and other teachers have observed about boys' schools is the level of aggression and violence in them. Many of the teachers we have talked to about working in boys' schools have expressed anxiety over this. Teachers in primary and mixed secondary schools have also talked to us about aggressive behaviour in boys. The general belief that men are more aggressive than women is perhaps the most common belief about differences between the sexes. It is probably also the one which is most commonly attributed to biological determinism rather than social construction. In staff-rooms we have commonly heard the opinion that the physicality between boys is not really aggressive but is 'play-fighting'. This seems to us closely related to other statements such as 'boys will be boys', or the unproblematic acceptance of 'Well, that's just how boys are'. The strange thing to us is that there seems to be an acceptance that boys are more aggressive naturally, and therefore it is *all right*. We would argue that *even if* boys were born with a natural inclination towards violence, that does not make it acceptable. After all, social conventions generally mean that many behaviours which by nature we might feel disposed towards are frowned on in society, and we have to restrain ourselves!

The evidence that boys/men do behave more aggressively than girls/women is strong. Bob Connell (1985) writes:

> Almost all the soldiers in the world are men. So are most of the police, most of the prison warders and almost all of the generals, admirals, bureaucrats and politicians who control the apparatuses of coercion and collective violence.
>
> Most murderers are men. Almost all bandits, armed robbers and muggers are men; all rapists, most domestic bashers; and most people involved in street brawls, riots and the like. The same story, then, for both organised and unorganised violence. It seems that there is some connection between being male and being violent ... It is also very important that much of the actual violence is not isolated and individual but it is institutional. Much of the poofter-bashing is done by police; much of the world's rape is done by soldiers in the context of war. These actions grow readily out of the 'legitimate' violence for which police forces and armies are set up.

The majority of reports dealing with aggression in young children have been concerned with nursery schools. They have also largely focused on middle-class boys (Archer and Lloyd 1982). In more than twenty investigations published before 1966, boys were observed to be more aggressive than girls. More recent studies in Britain have had similar results. One study carried out in fifteen different nursery schools and playgroups found that conflicts between boys were more frequent than conflicts between girls or between girls and boys (Smith and Green 1975). In a study of eleven-year-old boys and girls in the classroom, the boys showed more physical aggression than girls of the same age (Archer and Westman 1981).

In a study in California, four-year-old children were invited to play in groups of three — all of the same sex — on a trampoline in a room with a one-way mirror. A clear difference was found in the way the boys and girls played. About a quarter of the boys engaged in fairly extreme types of horseplay, piling on top of each other on the trampoline or rushing into each other. None of the girls played really boisterously. John Nicholson (1984) comments on this study:

> There does seem to be a sex difference in children's games, but
> two points must be borne in mind. The first, that even the most
> exuberant boys in the California study *were only fighting in fun*, so
> it would be rash to treat this as evidence that boys are more
> aggressive than girls (our emphasis).

His second point is that the rough-and-tumble play is actually
due to the behaviour of a small group of untypical boys.

It seems to us that whether or not boys only 'fight in fun' is
rather beside the point. If we accept that much of children's play
is a copy and a practice of adult roles, then this kind of 'play' is
worrying. And, although our classroom observations also
suggest that the number of boys engaged in aggressive
behaviour at any one time is small, it seems to us that a high
proportion of boys we have observed over extended periods of
time have exhibited aggressive behaviour *at some time or other*.
This is not true of the same proportion of girls observed over an
equal period of time. This reminds us of the times we have tried
to set up various role-play situations with groups of boys, and
then tried the same exercise with groups of girls. We have
realised over the years that, if it is at all possible for the role-play
to have a violent outcome that is, in all probability, how many
boys will interpret it. For example, the following situation was
provided for some pupils. Two pupils have had an argument in
the playground over who has the most expensive shoes. Two
volunteers take the role of pupils and the third plays a teacher
trying to calm down the situation and discuss with the pupils
why it should not have happened. What invariably happened
was that the two pupils started fighting and the 'teacher' joined
in! The situation, when presented to girls, never had the same
outcome.

Aggression has also been studied in children through the
questionable method of setting up a situation in the laboratory
where children think they can inflict pain on other children
without any risk of retaliation. In the experiments children have
been given a reason to use this power. In an experiment of this
kind, a group of eight-year-olds was told that a child in the next
room was working on a set of arithmetic problems, and asked to
help by pressing a button every time a wrong answer was given.
The button would mean the child would be hit with a punching-

machine. They were told this would help the child learn. The children were told from time to time that the 'victim' had made a mistake, and pressed buttons which were supposed to deliver blows ranging in power — number one, a soft punch; five, a medium punch; and ten, a hard punch. The boys chose to inflict significantly more pain than the girls on their non-existent victim. (Nicholson, 1984).

Questionnaires have been used with boys and girls to ask what they think about various situations involving violence and aggression; these have also shown that boys appear to be more aggressive than girls. It seems that boys think more aggressively and have a more aggressive image of themselves from these studies. (However, when girls have been rewarded with 'prizes' for beating up a doll, they have beaten it up as aggressively as the boys!)

Nicholson (1984) comments about studies comparing adult male and female levels of aggression.

> What really seems to hold women back is that they feel much more strongly than men that they ought not to behave aggressively, and become much more anxious after behaving aggressively unless they have some justification for their action … the circumstances in which women show aggression are very different; either there is a matter of principle involved, or else they see someone else treated unfairly.

There seem to us strong arguments to point to the social construction of male aggression. Firstly, even *if* a biological explanation is given, for example male levels of testosterone, there is evidence to show that hormones themselves are affected by the environment. For example, Rose *et al.* (1972) have found that when a monkey moves up the hierarchy by winning a fight and gaining in dominance, his testosterone level rises dramatically. The level of testosterone in the defeated monkey drops. It has also been found that emotional stress causes marked reductions in the levels of both male and female hormones in human beings (Archer 1979). Additionally, the greater aggressiveness of boys is observed from a very young age, from as young as two or three, long before the rise in testosterone levels at puberty. As we argued earlier, many of the toys seen as 'boys' toys' encourage physical activity, if not aggression. For example, guns, swords, action men, and the new, very popular, space models. Again, as we mentioned earlier, most of the male heroes in comics and on television (whether goodies or baddies) are violent.

Toughness and aggression are approved of in boys — the argument goes as follows: boys are encouraged to be tough and stick up for themselves. This is not usually meant as an open encouragement for them to be violent, but more of a message that violence is all right if not taken to extremes, that it is an appropriate way of 'looking after yourself' and can, in many circumstances, be a way of improving social status with other boys. Perhaps the most important message that boys learn is that they must at all costs avoid being thought to be afraid to fight. Boys also see members of their own gender engaging in violence, whereas girls generally do not. Boys may be rewarded with parental approval for being rough: 'I like the way he's rough. He's a proper lad', remarked one mother about her four-year-old son (Newson and Newson 1968).

Bob Connell (1985) argues in relation to the social construction of masculinity:

> War, murder, rape and masculinity are *cultural* facts not settled by biology. The patterns we have to deal with as issues of current politics have been produced within human society by the processes of history. It is the shape of social relations, not the shape of genes that is the effective cause. 'Male' and 'masculinity' are very different things. Masculinity is implanted in the male body; it does not grow out of it.

The main point we would like to make here is that aggression, whether 'in fun' or 'for real' *is* associated with masculinity in this society. Aggression in boys is a reflection of attitudes and beliefs about violence generally in society and it is, therefore, related to the nature of wider society and to the power relations between groups in it. Metcalf and Humphries (1985) argue that the popularisation of monetarist politics on both sides of the Atlantic has played upon a particular kind of masculinity:

> In the USA and Britain growing Western militarism has played on the most reactionary ideas of male sexuality ... President Reagan and Mrs Thatcher sell themselves as military leaders, the leaders of fighting men, real men, not wimps or wets.

Bob Connell also argues that:

> This connection between admired masculinity and violent response to threat is a resource that governments can use to mobilise support for war. A cult of masculinity and toughness flourished in the Kennedy and Johnson administrations in the USA and helped commit the country to war in Vietnam. I can remember the process operating on young men of my generation in Australia, whose Conservative government sent troops to support the Americans in Vietnam. Involvement in the war was presented as standing up to a threat, the opponents were smeared as lily-livered effeminates. In the fullness of time support for napalm raids and carpet bombing by B-52s became the test of manliness.

Aggression should not be seen as unproblematic and just a normal part of being male. We should be developing strategies to deal with aggression in school which take into account its gender implications and seek to challenge it in a more positive way (more positive than only reacting to violent incidents, when they occur, by a telling-off, suspension, calling in parents, and so on).[4]

Society encourages boys to behave aggressively. This does not mean that they are not responsible for their actions. The older they get, the less excusable are sexist acts of hostility and aggression which are aimed either towards one another or towards women. Schools should be places which challenge these patterns of aggression. As one male teacher put it: 'It's no good saying society makes men behave like that towards women. Men *allow themselves* to be kept in that role. We shouldn't deny our ability to change this. Male teachers, particularly, need to help boys by offering them another model as a way of being and behaving. Unfortunately, many men in schools do not offer this and do not see any reason for doing so'. In our experience, boys and men sometimes 'blame' women for their own aggressive sexist actions. For example, a woman teacher 'asked for it' or 'really deserved it', so they can be forgiven for 'giving it to them'. They shift responsibility for a sexist action onto others instead of accepting it themselves.

How do men and boys experience the pressures to be 'male'?

Hodson (1984) appears to be arguing that men are oppressed by sexism and that there is a need for 'male liberation'.

> Men are the super-sensitive sex. They feel threatened and are getting hurt, but won't accept it. They are in great need of stable relationships, but women are currently criticising, rejecting and divorcing them. Men are poor at intimacy. The rules of the power game have changed. Women are gaining equality with men.

Metcalf and Humphries (1985) observe that 'traditionally men have been quite at ease spouting off on any subject under the sun except one: themselves'. We do not regard men as being oppressed by sexism, but we do acknowledge that they may be prevented from reaching their full human potential because of it.

We are not primarily concerned in this book that because of socialisation boys and men find it difficult to talk about themselves. (In fact, we think it is erroneous to assume that girls and women can talk about themselves. We believe the opposite — that because of socialisation, girls and women are often very far removed from recognising their own feelings and needs, although they may be more tuned in to the feelings and needs of others.) In the same way, an assumption that women are gaining equality with men or that 'the rules of the power game have changed', we also believe to be false. *Some* women may have gained more equality with *some* men, but for the majority of women the rules have not changed and the power still resides very firmly in the hands of white, upper-middle-class males.

We go on to look at ways male socialisation may restrict the personal development of boys and men. This is very important because it often results not only in damage to the boys themselves, but can be even more destructive to the people they interact with and their relationship with their environment.

Several studies have been published in the last few years which are concerned with men's experiences and the adverse effect of male socialisation on men's lives. Morrison and Eardly (1985) believe that:

> Boys grow up to be wary of each other. We are taught to compete with one another at school, and to struggle to prove ourselves

outside it, on the street, the playground and the sportsfield. Later we fight for status over sexual prowess, or money, or physical strength or technical know-how. We fear to admit our weakness to one another, to admit our failures, our vulnerability, and we fear being called a cissy, a wet or a softy. The pressure is on to act tough. We fear humiliation or exclusion, or ultimately the violence of other boys if we fail to conform.

Vic Seidler (1980) supports this:

> As boys, we have to be constantly on the alert to either confront or avoid physical violence. We have to be ready to defend ourselves. We are constantly on our guard ... Masculinity is never something we can feel at ease with. It is always something we have to be ready to prove and defend.

Other similar studies focus on how men experience masculinity and describe the ways that it is problematic for men (Hodson 1984; Metcalf and Humphries 1985; Ingham 1984; Levinson 1978). Morrison and Eardley (1985), for instance, argue that male cameraderie often takes the place of and expresses men's deep desire for genuine friendship with other men; but that this cameraderie occurs in a context that is designed to put men in competition with one another. A contradiction emerges that is at once a reaching out and 'a keeping at bay'. Tolson (1977) reports the difficulty many men expressed over communicating. He found it was difficult for them to discuss any personal feelings with one another.

Boys have expressed similar feelings. Below are edited extracts from an interview originally recorded for *True Romance*. Gary and Dave were in the fifth form of a London comprehensive school at the time. Paul Morrison, who talks to them, describes them as 'exceptions' in terms of being able to find the 'strength to reject much of the power of "boys' world"'.

> Gary: That's a funny thing, really, because if a boy is close to another boy, it's sort of said: 'No man, this is a funny thing. Them two are too close, you know. They must be gay or something'. When two girls are close, they could walk down the street holding hands, everything's fine.
> Dave: But if two boys did the same, their names'd be mud in the school.

Gary: Yeah, because ... If I went into a room, right, the acceptable way to greet my friend was to punch him on the shoulder or shake hands, you know. But if a girl went into a room, they'd kiss each other on the cheek, or something like that.

...

Gary: If you've got a friend, it doesn't matter how long you've known him, you keep him at a distance, as a man. But you let the girl get close to you. I just don't see it as right. The only way you're meant to relate to a boy is if you're boasting. 'Cos you come into school and if you wanna say something to a guy you boast about it. You don't talk about your failures to him. You're not meant to do that. Your failures are meant to be kept in yourself.

Dave: You don't talk about your failures or shortcomings with girls, either. When you're with a girl you're supposed to be a Superman. Like I know a lot of boys, when they're on their own they're friendly to you, when they're with a girl they try to take you on or something — put on a veneer of super-hardness, try and pick a fight or something.

...

Paul: What is it that blokes don't talk about?

Gary: Their failures. That's basically it. Their failures.

In our work in schools with boys, several have described to us what it is like for them. Wayne, who is fourteen, and at a London mixed comprehensive, describes his experiences as follows:

In school most people are concerned with their image — most boys are expected to conform, to dress the same. They're supposed to be interested in football matches and beat up other people, and that's taken as fun. They especially beat up younger, smaller people. Anything extraordinary or unusual that you happen to do is taken as something from another planet. There's a lot of pressure on boys to be friends with popular boys. If you don't go around with them then you're treated as a weirdo. It's 'follow the leader'. If you don't see another boy outside school, you can't get to know what he's really like ...

There's a lot of pressure on kids to be fashionable. It has to be a certain style. You can only dress casually or trendy or punk if you're part of those groups ... It's hard if you want to get on in school because you're expected to participate in the messing about, especially if you're a boy.

Sean goes to a boys' school. He talks about how his behaviour is guarded in front of other boys:

> You have to be careful about what you let out about yourself. You get picked on for anything around here. You've got to be careful not to let the other kids think you're soft.

In this chapter we have suggested that there are considerable pressures on boys to behave in stereotyped masculine ways. One of the effects of this is that constraints operate in their interpersonal relationships with other boys. We have described some of the possible effects on their socialisation and absorption of stereotyped notions about girls and women. This socialisation process has important implications for the way boys learn, which we look at in the next chapter.

Notes

1 Boys are often perceived as a 'problem' in this sense in terms of discipline. It seems important, though, to ask which boys are thus perceived. If they are largely black, working-class boys then clearly there are classist and racist implications.
2 In one LEA a diagnostic centre for learning difficulties reports that approximately 75 per cent of children referred for problems with reading and writing are boys.
3 The twenty more commonly assigned adjectives characteristic of women found by Bem (1974) included childlike, gullible, shy, yielding, loyal and flatterable.
4 We would like to make a distinction between general aggression and violence which might be destructive to the boys themselves or others and the ability to express anger assertively and positively over a personal or political issue.

CHAPTER 2

Classroom Dynamics

Evidence from extensive classroom observations suggests that girls and boys may be involved in quite different learning processes at school. They may be learning different interests and skills, valuing various activities differently, and even using the same materials or activities in quite different ways. This may occur even when 'equal opportunities' are apparently available to both girls and boys. The evidence suggests that this starts very early.

Learning in primary schools

To explore boys' and girls' learning experiences in infant classes, we began by 'interviewing' infant children in a racially mixed Inner London primary school about their favourite activities. The children were individually presented with photographs of different activities and areas of their classroom as a basis for discussion. They talked about what toys they played with, how often, who else played with them, how they used them, and what they were most interested in. Some striking points arose from these discussions: all the boys were very enthusiastic about the photo of the lego, while only two girls said they played with it, when pressed, and three girls said they didn't like lego at all. Most children described lego as being used to make cars and houses — and said that boys made cars and girls made houses. Most boys described using the home corner in a variety of ways, for example, they pretended to be

18

dogs and jumped on the table and around the room. The girls used the home corner for more conventional domestic activities.

The picture that emerged time and again throughout the classrooms of primary schools we observed was one of boys being primarily involved *in an individualistic way* in processes of 'making', constructive play, physical manipulation and an expansive use of space. Alongside this, we commonly observed girls involved in various forms of social play and restrictive use of space. Girls and boys seemed to approach joint activities in very different ways. Girls tended to talk to each other about their activity as they went along. They would discuss how to organise their work; for example, break it up into different aspects and decide who would do which, or work out what was necessary for preparation. Boys tended to talk together about things not related to the activity they were engaged in, talking about it only when absolutely necessary or when a conflict arose. In fact, conflicts concerning joint work arose very much more frequently with boys than with girls. Here are two 'typical' examples of girls and of boys working together:

Two girls were painting a joint picture (a large snail in the garden). They decided what colours they wanted and shared mixing the paints. They decided who should draw the outline (and why) and they proceeded to divide various aspects of the picture for each to do. There was discussion throughout the session about how the picture was coming on, how things looked, colours, and so on.

Two boys were painting a joint picture (a road with shops behind it). One boy insisted on drawing the outline. Then each boy took charge of painting one half of the picture. When one boy, who was painting the road, came to the middle of the page, he painted a careful vertical line down the middle of the road and stopped. Talk between the boys was about an episode on the playground and the only time they discussed the painting was when one boy didn't like the way the other painted the shops — then conflict arose and the second boy stopped painting.

It is not enough to devise certain learning strategies without also taking into consideration the different ways that boys and girls may engage in them. When setting up our own collaborative learning situations, for instance, we found that boys tended not to collaborate, but to work independently.

A number of interesting studies have highlighted the different ways in which boys and girls approach collaborative tasks. For example, a small-scale research survey undertaken by Davis and Ticher (1986) with a group of reception-aged infants in a school in East London, was primarily set up for the purpose of looking more closely at how groups of reception children use construction materials. Jonathan Ticher, the class teacher, and Jenny Davis, a consultant mathematics teacher, noticed early on that the boys were choosing construction materials, especially lego, more often than girls, and were making more elaborate models with it. In order to look at the processes involved they videotaped a group of four girls and four boys who were given the following problems to solve with large-size lego: (a) how to build a 'house', and (b) how to build a tall structure. The four girls worked together constructing an enclosed space. Two boys, working on a separate wall, decided they would like to join their wall to the girls' house. The boys then assumed control of the building and directed the girls to bring them bricks. The group was then asked to make their structure 'tall' instead. The girls did this by standing on chairs and passing bricks to one another. The boys first copied this, then knocked down the girls' structure and took their bricks. The next week a different group was given the same task. This time the girls began collaboratively to build their house without discussion among themselves, the boys began work on four individual constructions. 'Several wonky piles of bricks resulted', while the girls quickly built a wall that was as tall as themselves and were expanding it vertically and horizontally. When the bricks began to run out the boys started taking bricks from each other's structures until a fight ensued and a teacher intervened. The girls again worked collaboratively on the 'tall' structure. The boys began to lose interest in their task and drifted away. Davis and Ticher comment:

> This re-emphasised for us just how important the feeling of 'being in control' is in the learning process. The children who opted out could have felt inhibited by others who had greater competence than they had. Once another child had taken over, whether pleasantly or by force, the excluded children seemed to lack the will to negotiate their way back into the activity.

Davis and Ticher realised that they were mistaken in assuming a deficit model in relation to girls' constructional abilities. They were interested to see what happened when the girls from the two different groups came together without boys. Immediately there was a noticeable sense of freedom and more talk. After some initial building near the beginning 'an elaborate fantasy play began: one girl became the mother and went to cook in the kitchen. An outside girl was bodily lifted in and her inclusion was reinforced by her being chosen as the cat, given food, stroked and petted in a display of affection and tenderness'. In answer to their initial question, Davis and Ticher wonder whether the difference in use of constructional materials had something to do with both the nature of the materials offered to children and with the different ways those materials are seen. They suggest, for example, that because lego is very small and abundant in most classrooms it tends to encourage small, individual work rather than collaborative work (which girls seem to prefer). This research, although small-scale, reinforces the idea that the gender differences between boys and girls will have serious implications for learning in school and that expectations of gender behaviour will have been internalised at an early age. (One of the interesting things to have emerged from our discussions with teachers is that the differences in behaviour between boys and girls are as noticeable at five as at fifteen.)

The observations which we made of primary school playgrounds were consistent with the sorts of behaviour we were seeing in the classroom. In general, we observed that, for the most part, boys dominated the playground space and were engaged in active, physical pursuits, while girls often occupied the peripheries or the 'quiet' playground space (where provided) together with the smaller children. Many boys were commonly engaged in physically manipulative play which utilised a large area, while many girls played games not requiring much space and talked together constantly as part of their activity. These observations have been corroborated by many discussions with primary teachers.

In both playground and the classroom, competitiveness was another feature which constantly permeated many boys' activities (be it physical sport, whose model went faster, who was further along in their maths book, or who was on a 'higher' level in their work). Even collaborative activities which required team work were organised and approached in such a way that competition became a key feature of the activity. Our observations of the girls usually showed the opposite — almost any activity provided a chance to collaborate, discuss, assist and interact generally.

In one classroom small groups of boys and girls were engaged in an activity making cylinders of various sizes and seeing how much weight they could take. Each group was asked to describe the task to one of us as a newcomer to the classroom. The girls' group described the task in purely descriptive terms, and also described how they had helped each other to make the cylinder, load it with weights and record how much it could take. Without exception, the boys' groups described the task in competitive terms (for example, 'to see who can make the strongest cylinder' or 'to see who can use the most weights').

As we have said, we observed that certain areas of the classroom and playground tended to be dominated by the boys. This territorial attitude extended even to certain classroom activities which were not primarily related to considerations of space. Certain materials, such as lego and other constructional toys, and anything to do with science, seemed to be regarded by the boys as 'theirs'. This was evident not only in the number of boys doing these activities, but also in the ways the boys behaved towards the girls. If, during a class project which involved the use of items such as scales, measures or stop watches, the boys ran out of these materials, they would commonly simply take them from girls, despite the fact that the girls were using them. In the main, the girls we observed who were 'pushed out' or 'taken over' behaved quite deferentially towards these boys. Some girls complained, some would fight back, but we saw the latter less commonly. We wondered if this behaviour, in part, reflected the fact that the girls perceived the boys as having a greater right to use these materials. The question of how definitions or assumptions of what type of knowledge, activity or behaviour belongs to whom has direct implications for what we learn.

It could be that the way many girls accept boys monopolising certain areas of the classroom has to do with their more pressing desire for a 'quiet life' and a peaceful atmosphere. Pat Mahoney (1985) attributes the apparent passivity of some girls towards boys as being a 'strategy' in itself, a way of coping that works best for themselves in that situation. We remember that, as children, many of 'us girls' simply did not take the boys seriously. We disdained their 'showing off' and 'being silly', and were dismissive about their 'immature behaviour'. We wonder if some of what appears as passive accommodation in girls could reflect, in fact, a 'can't be bothered with you' attitude.

It seemed to us that boys have a greater need than girls to identify certain activities as male or female. A consequence of this seemed to be that boys would often not only assume dominance over activities they have identified as 'male', but also avoid those identified as 'female'. Furthermore, not only do many boys bring competition into almost all activities they engage in, but also it is the competition which seems to become the fundamental source of motivation.

It may well be that because of boys' monopoly of classroom activities, girls may not be getting the same grounding in mechanical, physical and three-dimensional skills. Girls score lower on tests measuring spatial reasoning and problem-solving. The Cockcroft Report (1982) shows that boys scored significantly better than girls on tests requiring spatial ability; and on more complex items requiring abstract thought; problem-solving; conceptualisation. (Girls were found to score better on tasks requiring rule-following.) Spatial visualisation in itself is often taken to be particularly crucial to the comprehension of mathematics. However, statistics about sex-related differences in mathematics are themselves contentious, as Walden and Walkerdine (1982) have shown.

It has been claimed that the reasons girls under-achieve in mathematics are social, to do with unequal opportunities at school, low expectations by teachers, and lack of positive role models. All those things are likely to affect girls' interest, confidence and aspirations, especially in combination with the messages of non-entitlement they often receive from boys' domination of these areas in school. But is there not another important factor also affecting girls' and boys' learning? The way that girls, by and large, do not have the same opportunities to develop constructional and manipulative skills because of boys' domination of activities which facilitate this. It is reasonable to suppose therefore, that girls may not be developing the same conceptual framework, and that this in turn puts them at a further disadvantage in certain areas of mathematics and science.

Boys, on the other hand, usually do less well than girls on verbal reasoning tests and, later in their school careers, achieve less well in, and opt less for, English and modern languages. In 1982, 18,000 more boys than girls left school with no qualification in English, 10,000 more girls than boys achieved pass grades in O level English or equivalent.

Generally, boys have limited verbal interaction, and use language less than girls. Similarly, a study of the behaviour of nine-year-old boys and nine-year-old girls at the University of Denver, Colorado reported that:

> In practically every case, the boys ignored each other as people. They displayed no personal curiosity. They did not look at each other's faces. They didn't ask personal questions. They didn't volunteer information about themselves. Conversation was confined to the technical problems of lego-design. In every essential respect, the boys stayed solitary and played by themselves.   (Hodson 1984)

In contrast, the girls revealed three times as much about themselves as did the boys. Afterwards, it was discovered that the girls liked each other more as a result of their greater efforts towards getting to know each other. The boys remained mutually indifferent.

Although we are describing learning differences between girls and boys, we are in no way describing differences in *capacities* for learning. This is an important point; our examination of learning differences is entirely in terms of 'how' and 'why'. We suggest that differences in girls and boys may go deep, and so it is important not only to look at discrepancies in achievement terms, but also to look at the actual processes of mental, emotional and physical development in terms of gender.

Boys do not aspire to 'caring' roles or professions which are traditionally female spheres. Our observations suggest that there is very little time in school when boys are able to 'rehearse' skills of personal interaction, intimate communication and caring or co-operative behaviour, as girls do. They are not developing, in the main, the same skills, interest in or even valuation of these areas. Furthermore, because activities and play related to these activities are identified as 'female', such behaviour may well be avoided or considered not appropriate 'masculine' behaviour.

General issues in relation to gender and learning

In our opinion, early socialisation and sex-stereotyped attitudes about boys and girls have a fundamental effect on the *processes* of education in relation to teaching style and methodology and the way in which learning is negotiated by boys and girls. For instance, we were recently told by the head of a Learning Difficulties Diagnostic Centre that 'somewhere between 70 and 80 per cent of pupils referred to us are boys'. Boys are referred to Diagnostic Centres mainly for problems with reading.

Barrs and Pidgeon (1986) report that gender differences in patterns of reading are of increasing concern to teachers. They argue that there are sharp and observable differences between boys and girls as readers. Both in terms of reading *ability* and in terms of the *amount* of voluntary reading, girls consistently read *better* and *more* than boys. A primary school survey by the Assessment of Performance Unit (1983) noted that 'girls achieved higher mean scores in reading and writing than did boys'. More detailed evidence came from the ILEA Junior Survey (1985), which showed differences between boys and girls in terms of average reading scores both on entry to junior school and in the fourth year. It could be assumed that the sex stereotyped portrayal of the world presented by the great majority of books for young children, would mean that girls would be less successful readers. Barrs and Pidgeon offer compelling reasons why this is not so. Firstly, although boys are shown engaging in many different activities in books, one activity they are not shown doing is reading, nor taking part in any other quiet or thoughtful activity.

In addition, Barrs and Pidgeon suggest that 'girls and boys

must begin to develop views of themselves as potential readers when they are quite small, and the adults around them are likely to be a major influence on the self concepts in this, as in other respects'.

It is interesting to speculate that boys' slower development in reading might also relate to the differences observed between girls and boys in their ways of interacting with others. Girls' greater reliance on verbal skills for social interaction might give them an advantage when they begin to learn to read. It may also mean that girls place a greater value on language-based activity. In addition to difficulties in learning to read, it has been shown that the reading matter of boys and girls is quite different. Surveys (for example, Whitehead's report 'Children and their books', 1977) have consistently shown that boys read more non-fiction than girls. Non-fiction gives access to external knowledge, 'facts', and information, while fiction is concerned with the lives, thoughts and feelings of other people. This choice of reading matter fits well with what is known of early socialisation of boys and girls. And of course, reading of any kind is a passive activity.

Ways in which boys and girls may internalise gender expectations in their learning were highlighted by an experiment by Hargreaves (1983). He showed that males and females may only have to *think* that a task will be performed better by the opposite sex to do badly at it. Hargreaves asked 38 boys and 38 girls to play with a 'wiggly wire'. This is a game sometimes found at school fêtes where the object is to pass a wire loop all the way down a wiggly wire without touching it. If you touch the wire a bell rings. Hargreaves told half the children that this was a test to see how good they would be at mechanics or operating machinery, and the other half that it would test how good they were at needlework, sewing and knitting. Compared to the number of errors the children made when they were given instructions 'appropriate' for their sex, both boys and girls did significantly worse on the task if they thought the game tested a skill that was the 'prerogative' of the opposite sex. 'So apparent sex differences in certain abilities', Hargreaves says, 'may be even less ingrained than people think'.

Teachers' responses to their pupils can also provide strong messages about the type of behaviour and ways of working that are most valued, and these often relate to gender stereotypes. Walden and Walkerdine (1985) looked into the criteria teachers used for entering girls and boys for an O level mathematics course. Although the fourth-year girls outperformed the boys in the test they administered, many more boys than girls were entered. They found that teachers felt that 'male' characteristics such as haphazardness, rule-breaking and challenging the teacher on maths problems accompanied 'flair', 'brilliance' or 'real understanding'. At the same time, 'female' characteristics, such as conscientiousness, neatness and co-operation, led teachers to suspect a lack of 'real understanding' and mere 'rule-following'. Their study begs a closer look at what sorts of trait teachers (unconsciously?) associate as desirable with certain subjects and how these may in fact be stereotyped traits which are gender related.

Just as certain assumptions may be made about a child on the basis of gender, class assumptions may also be made. Ideas about criteria for success are often linked to middle-class traits (such as ways of speaking) so that it is these class traits themselves which become associated as accompanying and necessary for success.

This also operates in racist ways. There is now evidence that teachers perceive the same behaviour in different ways, depending on whether a child is white or black. The Eggleston Report (1986) showed that some white teachers seemed to perceive certain behaviour in black boys as more threatening than the same sort of behaviour in white boys. These teachers responded differently to these boys in their lessons according to their ethnic group.

We are likely to internalise the dominant stereotypes about race, class or gender qualities and characteristics of pupils. We work in institutions which reflect the inequalities in society in terms of the dominance and power of some groups. We need to guard against stereotypical assumptions that affect our expectations of pupils. Steve Goldenberg (1986) writes: 'The term (under-achievement) assumes the existence of equality of opportunity and that all students are striving for the same success, which they can achieve on a purely meritocratic basis whatever their place in the socio-economic structure'. He argues that this does not take into account the way the education system privileges the already privileged and ignores the initial inequalities. Several teachers interviewed by Goldenberg were conscious of a disparity in their attitudes towards the classroom behaviour of middle- and working-class pupils:

> The tutor set think I give more attention (to a group of middle-class girls) in two ways, both in terms of their work and how I treat their behaviour. And I think it does influence me that, because I know they are nice girls, I do let them off the hook sometimes, and I shouldn't.

Expectations about *ability* as construed in terms of behaviour are also apparent in this girl's explanation about why she was in a CSE rather than an O level class:

> It's who she likes. If you are a big mouth who likes to back-chat her, she chucks you in the CSE and if you're a softy, you know, listen and don't talk a lot, she puts you in the 'O' level. You know I think that's how she done it. (Riley 1985)

Riley writes that most of the black girls she interviewed had been placed in the CSE group. The interrelationship of classist, racist and sexist assumptions and expectations about children in school seems to us highly complex. For example, we cannot talk only about teacher expectations and *sexism* in the system contributing to boys' success in sciences in comparison to girls'. In a school we visited recently the Physics O level class was made up of about 60 per cent white, middle-class boys, and about 30 per cent white, middle-class girls. The CSE science class was made up of mainly black and working-class children. Another example is the high proportion of black boys removed from main stream schools and marginalized into 'special schools'.

Many of the boys we have talked to in schools have expressed unhappiness in relation to the position they find themselves in. Wayne complained, and two others in his class concurred, that

> The boys get in trouble more than the girls. It's the boys that always get told off. The girls get more treats and are asked to go with the register more or do something responsible.

Additionally they all felt that it was the black boys who received most of the negative attention.

Boys in mixed secondary classrooms

There is considerable evidence that boys demand the greater proportion of teacher attention, in both primary and secondary school. Boys' monopoly of physical space, use of facilities and teachers' time in secondary school is well documented and is not essentially different from primary school observations. Carricoates' (1978) interviews with primary school teachers about teaching girls and boys brought consistent comments such as: 'The boys are more difficult to settle down to their work ... they don't seem to have the same self-discipline that girls do'. 'It's a bit harder to keep the boys' attention during the lesson'. 'Boys are more difficult to control. It's more important to keep their attention ... otherwise they play you up something awful'. Stanworth (1981), Walkerdine (1981) and Fuller (1980) have all pointed to the extent of boys' domination of the mixed classroom in secondary school: their noisiness; their demands that lesson content be interesting and directed at them; the need for discipline. Tingle (1985) writes about his experience as an English teacher of boys being amalgamated into a girls' school:

> The boys plunge into things, interrupt discussion, can't keep still, can't wait. Ten boys in a class of 29 and they demand 50% or more of my time. Yet the work they produce is often shallow, non-reflective and is always messy ... The boys, in protective groups, generally resist giving anything of themselves. They hide their feelings, they joke, they are loud, they are very physical.

Margaret Sandra's (1985) research also reveals ways in which boys can cause continual disruption within the classroom. She was principally concerned with why boys consistently under-achieved in English. She observed classes in the ILEA with the intention of exploring whether it was possible to map any differences in girl/boy performance in English. Initially, she taped lessons but it soon became apparent to her that verbal responses were only a tiny fraction of the ways in which pupils are caught into sex-differentiated behaviour affecting learning. She listed all activities she saw pupils engaged in during lessons and used this to create an observation chart. Certain activities could clearly be identified with one sex or the other, the most disruptive behaviour being male. Here are some of them:

Girls	Boys
hand-up	pencil tapping
chewing	calling out
reading	bag on table
make-up	shove ha'penny
brushing hair	misusing material
showing work to teacher	

In addition, boys were more likely to arrive late in the classroom and to be poorly equipped.

French (1986) suggests that the way boys disrupt a lesson in which they are not interested might lead teachers to gear lesson content to the boys as a means of imposing discipline. Boys also appear to exert control over the classroom through direct intimidation of the girls. Pat Mahoney (1985) observed classes and interviewed girls and boys in three inner-city secondary schools. She concludes that boys control the mixed classroom by dominating the girls physically as well as verbally. She believes this provides a means of proving masculinity for boys in mixed schools. (This concurs with our observations in primary schools where we have observed a 'low-level', on-going harassment of girls by some boys. This took the form of 'put-downs', comments about girls' work or ability, needling and 'wind-up', tapping, poking, touching with feet when sitting on the floor, knocking down girls' work, taking over equipment girls are using, as well as overt forms of intimidation. 'Blaming' was another often observed behaviour, which seemed to result in some girls adopting a defensive deferential stance in relation to certain boys.)

Teachers said that most girls requiring their assistance will generally sit with their hand up or come over to them (and if the teacher is not free hover nearby, without speaking), while boys often shout out from across the room for assistance. Teachers talked about their own determination not to respond, but nevertheless, they continuously found themselves looking up or answering the 'summons'.

But beyond these overt ways of boys demanding teacher attention or claiming dominance in the classroom, it is also clear that boys claim a great deal of their teachers' time and attention simply as a result of their approach to their schoolwork, and the dynamics between themselves. Because of the preference for 'doing', 'making', 'handling' and 'manipulating' shown by so many boys, there seems to be a real reluctance towards undertaking other sorts of task. For example, after a science activity boys in one classroom we observed made it clear that being told by their teacher to 'put the scales away and write up the experiment' was perceived as a *punishment*. Making sure that boys complete assignments, conclude activities, write up experiments and even see through games that they've started, appears to take a great deal of teacher attention in the form of constant coaxing and cajoling, tempting, insisting and threatening. Additionally, a certain amount of teacher time also seems to be taken up mediating conflict between boys.

Boys-only groups

We have written about the ways in which boys learn to identify certain spheres of activity, knowledge and behaviour as masculine or feminine and value them accordingly. We have also shown why there is every reason to believe this begins long before secondary school. We have discussed evidence which suggests boys may dominate physical space and teacher time and attention, have greater difficulty in collaborating and relating personally; and may measure their own worth or success by direct competition with other boys. Certainly these types of behaviour, already so evident in primary school, seem to continue and polarise in secondary school. The curriculum itself is more clearly polarised into 'male' and 'female' subjects, with option choices and exam results reflecting this. (Of those entered for woodwork and metalwork O level in summer 1980, 99 per cent were boys. The corresponding figures for the other subjects were: physics, 77 per cent; mathematics, 60 per cent; economics, 59 per cent; geography, 56 per cent; art, 44 per cent; French, 41 per cent; biology, 37 per cent; sociology, 27 per cent; needlework, 0 per cent.)

Observing girls and boys in the mixed classroom can illuminate their learning of different skills, their different interests, expectations and behaviour and the different influences in their environments and development. It is also valuable to look at boys in all-boy settings in order further to illuminate the dynamics between them; the ways they may be relating to their school environment; ways they may be internalising the social context they operate within; and the ways boys learn.

Power dynamics and competition among boys in boys' schools

We referred earlier to the research by Pat Mahoney (1985) in which she observed classes and interviewed girls and boys in three inter-city comprehensive schools, and concluded that boys control the mixed classroom by dominating the girls physically as well as verbally. She suggested that this provides a means of proving masculinity for boys in mixed schools. Mahoney argues that as boys' schools lack this opportunity, masculinity has to be proved in another way, usually in terms of physical strength, which results in more physical violence. We agree with this, but our experience also agrees with Spender (1982) who reports some teachers' comments on single-sex boys' classrooms:

> It seems to me that the boys create an inferior or outside group and level the abuse at them that they would otherwise direct at girls. The least 'manly' boys become the target and are used as substitute girls in a way.

> In an all-boys' school a group of 'not real boys' gets created. They are called the poofters and the cissies and are constantly likened to girls. The sexual hierarchy gets set up but some boys have to play the part that the girls would take in a mixed school.

In one boys' school this was very overt. In one class, the boy who took on the role of 'girl' was even known as 'Janice'. All the boys called him 'Janice' most of the time and some teachers were heard to refer to him as 'Janice'. It seems clear that the boys' behaviour in classes we observed, while superficially directed against girls or against the teacher, is in fact directed at each other. They are proving through their behaviour that they are, in fact, 'real men' and very dependent on one another's approval. Pat Mahoney (1985) also wrote about this:

> What seems to emerge from this is that, contrary to popular myth about the independence of boys, they are in fact highly dependent on others. Yet there seem to be two sorts of

dependence at issue — boys' attempts to impress girls are not the same as their attempts to impress other boys. In the one case, girls are needed to provide servicing; whereas, in the other, boys depend on other boys for their identities as men.

Servicing, Mahoney explains, includes such things as girls providing boys with rulers, pens, and so on, and helping with homework, sorting out arguments, and generally making them feel 'nice'.

Boys in boys' schools confirm their identity as males through physical aggression and violence (or sometimes by their behaviour to women teachers: see Chapter 4). It appears that boys' behaviour to girls in mixed schools and much of adult male behaviour to women (for example, a group of men whistling at a woman) is a confirmation of their masculinity aimed at *each other*. The fact that boys themselves would prefer to go to mixed schools is confirmed in an EOC Report (1982): 'less homosexuality (top of the list), getting on with girls, less pressure to conform to macho images'. This same report also said that 'staff would certainly agree that there is less violence'. Pat Mahoney concludes from this:

> It is perhaps possible to theorise not that boys' schools construct masculinity more strongly but that it is reinforced in different ways. In mixed schools boys confirm their masculinity to each other through their behaviour towards girls, but in the absence of girls they may resort to physical violence to achieve their position in the male hierarchy ... That boys are so violently homophobic perhaps bears witness to the fact that they see each other as masculine if their sexuality is being practised on girls.

There follows an analysis of data we have compiled from classrooms observed in a boys' school over a two-year period; observations of a variety of lessons in a large number of other boys-only groups in other schools, extensive discussion with individual teachers and in-service workshops and conferences on working with boys. Our research focused on issues to do with the ways boys interrelate. For example, the things we concentrated on included both observing and asking about collaborative learning activities, the ways boys relate to each other, to men and women teachers, to different subjects and to different teaching methodologies. The sorts of issue that arose are central to the teaching of boys and their behaviour at school.

Boys Don't Cry

We observed a 'continuous power play' underlying most interactions between boys, an ongoing process of positioning and a continual seeking of status and prestige. This competitive behaviour not only operates at explicit levels, but also implicitly. It not only permeates social interaction but also affects approaches to most school activity. In our study many teachers complained that boys may be preoccupied with each other to the point where it affects practically everything they do, including their concentration and performance in their work and their relationships with the teachers. This seems especially true in the lower school where boys are new to the school or still smaller physically and in a more vulnerable position.

In many classrooms of eleven- and twelve-year-old boys there was continual competitive interaction among many of the boys. This could relate to their work, skill, dress, behaviour or activities, feats or fights outside the classroom. Boys seemed to be constantly attempting to impress each other through various antics in the classroom (which might involve provocative behaviour or rudeness towards the teacher) or generally 'winding' each other up, resulting in physical violence from time to time.

The ways girls and boys learn to develop self-esteem appeared largely to derive from different sources. It is true that there is also a competitive element in some of the ways girls develop self-esteem. From the time they are old enough to view themselves as female objects (and there is evidence to suggest this happens when they are quite young) girls are encouraged to assess and value themselves in terms of their physical appearance. Notions of 'beauty' exist within narrowly defined perimeters, and in direct comparison to other girls. In this sense, girls may learn to derive their self-esteem through a competitive relationship with other girls. But, because of the 'norms' of femininity (such as the 'caring' role), girls also learn to derive their self-esteem in ways to do with how supportive and helpful they are to others, in other words, not only through comparison in directly competitive terms, but also in a 'complementary' role to others. However, after observing and working with boys we suggest that, for boys, this sort of competitive basis to self-esteem goes very much deeper, starting much earlier, and is bound up with not only their appearance but their general performance throughout their lives. In our belief it relates, in some way, to the concept of the 'hero', reflecting the notion of a 'superior' male. In order to be 'the hero' of their own fantasy play or, indeed, a worthy male in their own lives, they must not merely possess certain qualities (for example, honour, bravery, strength) but must be superior in these to other boys. It is in this sense that the competitive dynamic among boys involves the development of masculine identity. Social divisions are being played out at a variety of different levels and of course gender is just one of them. School reflects this in its hierarchical organisation, its structures, its values and beliefs. (Chapter 3 deals with this in more detail.)

Modes of communication among boys

The boys in our study (who were from a variety of cultural, ethnic and class backgrounds) seemed largely to depend upon rigid, stylised and competitive ways of relating to one another within the classroom. Alongside the ongoing 'power-play' (and as a result of it?) most of the boys we observed demonstrated a general lack of trust and support towards each other. Unless they had been in classes where teachers had spent a long time deliberately developing relationships among the pupils, they, unlike girls, were unwilling to say things in front of each other which were personal or left them at all vulnerable. They were, for the most part, guarded towards each other and their talk revolved around impersonal subject matter. While boys would willingly and enthusiastically discuss the rights or wrongs of a particular political issue (for example, nuclear war) they were overwhelmingly unwilling to discuss their own behaviour, feelings or lives with each other. Furthermore, even when working together on a shared or collaborative task, talk was often restricted to either a minimal utilitarian exchange or else about something totally external and unrelated. It seemed as though they were unable or unwilling to use talk as a way of sharing experiences. Teachers we interviewed concurred with our observation: 'I've sometimes tried to do the same kind of discussion work in boy-only and girl-only groups with very different results. The girls always seem far more comfortable when discussing their own experiences'. 'I used to work in a girls' school. I've noticed at this boys' school that collaborative activities that worked with the girls don't work with the boys'.

There was considerable non-verbal, aggressive or physical communication among boys. 'Body language', such as stance or tone of voice, played a large part in interaction. Physicality was not only used as a means of intimidation between the boys, but also as a way of making social contact. It was not unusual to see a boy, walking past another, reach out and deliver a little 'punch' as a way of saying 'hello'. Conflicts, such as whose turn it was to use some materials, or how to go about a joint task, would often be expressed and decided in physical terms (for example, by a 'push' and 'shove'). Demands for teacher attention or classroom disruptions (intended or unintentional) were often in physical terms (such as tapping, banging or other noise-making tactics). A good deal of talk among boys in the classroom was to do with issuing challenges or 'put-downs' to each other.

We also repeatedly observed how difficult many boys seemed to find listening to one another. They would meet each other's statements with contradiction, comparison, derision or direct challenge. More often, they would simply not bother to listen, especially if they had something they themselves wished to say.

These observations clearly relate to our earlier findings, from our primary school observations, and other research about communications and gender. In our view, it has much to do with the pressures to erect and then protect a 'masculine' façade of hardness, toughness, imperviousness to pain and 'objective' unemotionality.

It probably also involves the rigorous denial of anything identified as 'female' within themselves (and this may well include certain types of social and verbal interaction). However, in terms of the dynamics between boys which result from these pressures, it seems to acquire a 'life of its own'. The more boys present this exterior, the more impossible it must become for them to relate to each other in other ways. The more boys take every opportunity to demonstrate their own superior 'masculine' qualities, by pouncing on another boy's weakness, the more dangerous it becomes to express any vulnerability in front of each other. Boys 'need' to keep their emotional distance from each other, perhaps because they are afraid of each other and of their own emotionality — lest they appear soft!

Bullying and aggression

Much that we have described so far comes under the heading of non-explicit aggressive behaviour. However, there is also a great deal of explicitly aggressive behaviour among boys at schools. Our observations in a variety of schools indicate that boys from all social classes and ethnic groups are involved in bullying or aggressive behaviour. Additionally, there was much racist bullying specifically affecting children from black and ethnic minority groups.

Apart from physical bullying we have heard a great amount of verbal abuse so common as to become part of 'normal' speech. Clearly much of the verbal abuse was homophobic, since much was done and said by boys which seemed to be based on the need to prove that they were not homosexual and that they despised homosexuality. If a boy physically touched another boy in any way other than aggressively he was likely to be called a 'poof' or 'queer'. In discussion with a first-year class of boys we asked whether they had wanted to come to a boys' school. Every boy in the class said 'no'. When asked why, one boy said he was worried his friends would think he was 'queer'. Another actually said he was worried that he would *become* 'queer' at the school. This attitude and the subsequent behaviour reinforces oppression of gay people and especially gay boys and pupils in the school. It also ensures the continuation of an aggressive social relationship, reinforces 'norms' of 'masculinity' and reflects the degree and urgency with which boys must actively defend this masculine identity. It seemed as though one of the most virulent insults that could be directed at most boys (judging by the strength of their reaction) was to be called 'soft' or 'wimp' or 'poof', 'coward' or something to that effect. This sort of insult usually resulted in the 'necessity' to retaliate aggressively in order to demonstrate the untruth of the accusation. Indeed, the insult itself often seemed to be issued as provocation or as a 'signal' for aggression.

Equally common was abuse describing female sex organs, 'cunt' being the most common. Curiously this seemed acceptable to most boys and did not cause any particular retaliation. An exception was when this form of abuse was used against mothers. This led to the boy defending his mother's honour and, by inference, his own, and sometimes to physical violence.

Bullying among boys at school, both within and outside the classroom, appeared to be chronic. Almost all the teachers we met complained about it. Pupils, too, frequently mentioned bullying:

Paul: There are some boys in the class who are always proving how hard they are. I haven't had a fight for a while, but if any one does bother me I'm ready to beat them up although I don't like fighting.

Derek: I keep a low profile, keep myself to myself really. There's always some kind of trouble going on, but I keep out of it if I can.

We suggest that to some extent it is bound up with 'acting out' the power structures within the school itself (and in wider society). One dimension of bullying has to do with the way physical power and strength are part of stereotyped male attributes. Bullying is a major way in which boys are able to demonstrate their manliness. Even though a boy might be physically weaker than another, to be able to 'take it like a man' is usually considered to be a good second-best masculine quality. In this sense, bullying can be seen as a manifestation of pressures put on boys to conform to male stereotypes. While we acknowledge that bullying also takes place among girls, we do not regard it as a gender issue in the same way. It conflicts with, rather than reinforces, stereotyped notions of 'femininity'.

Bullying is also a gender issue because of its implications for the ways in which males may relate to each other and to women in particular. The status given to the strong and the lack of status given to the weak creates power structures which are also reflected in male–female relationships. Stereotyped 'norms' encourage a dominant male role. (For example, the 'hen-pecked' husband is the butt of much humour.) Bullying becomes one way of gaining or expressing power and dominance over women.

In a boys' school there may be an increase in the extent of bullying among boys because it is an all-male environment. If it is true that weaker boys 'take the place' of girls at boys' schools by providing a 'butt' for proving masculinity, then perhaps bullying should not be regarded as essentially different from sexual harassment. It may be that it is simply a different expression of a power-play underlining both. The need to confirm aspects of 'masculinity' which involve competitive definitions of strength and power (perhaps especially exacerbated in the strong male ethos of the boys' schools) must be recognised as an element involved in attempts to explain the extent of violence by boys in school. Additionally, Suleiman and Suleiman (1985) argue that boys' response to competitive situations in the school may be with racist and sexist abuse, threats and physical violence.

Strangely, there seems to have been little research into the gender implications of bullying and violence in schools.[1] The fact that there is a need for research which will add to our understanding of bullying and violence in schools *is* supported by the findings of some small-scale surveys that have been conducted by LEAs. While not looking into the *type* of bullying, these have shown, for example, that in ILEA 22 per cent of the parents of eleven-year-olds identify bullying as a problem for their children. John and Elizabeth Newson (1984) also found bullying a problem in their account of the upbringing of 700 Nottingham children. Over one quarter of the parents of eleven-year-olds they interviewed knew their children were being bullied. Olweus (1978) found that bullying is two to three times more common among boys than girls. Many more boys than the 22 per cent reported in the ILEA study may be affected by bullying at school. When observing classes where bullying was actually taking place, we noticed that even if children were not directly affected (as the bully or the bullied) the fact that bullying was going on was very clearly recognised by all the boys in the class, and this put many constraints on everyone's behaviour — they had to 'watch their step' constantly in case they were the next victim, as our interviews with boys show. In addition, as parents, we both know of various occasions where our own children have been seriously bullied in school. Although we both initially reported incidents to the respective schools, neither of us liked the way it was handled and have not reported some subsequent incidents.

Boys' attitudes to teaching methods

In our own experience and the experience of the many teachers we have conferred with, certain teaching methods have fairly predictable outcomes in boys' classrooms. Some types of discussion and collaborative teaching methods are particularly difficult with boys. The difficulties relate to the sorts of observation we have made concerning ways in which boys communicate their competitive behaviour, the types of activity they identify as 'male' or 'female' and related valuation of these. Boys' expectations and perceptions of what is 'appropriate' education derive from the 'norms' and values of the school itself. These are discussed in Chapter 3.

There is a strong notion among many boys of what constitutes 'real work' and what does not. 'Real work' is usually written work. It is *product*-orientated. It is instantly recognisable as being about a particular subject, especially if it is a 'real' subject such as science or mathematics. Furthermore, most boys do not seem to regard talk-related activities as 'real' work.

While girls may also have a low opinion of the 'worth' of these activities in terms of school achievement, they will probably also value them as appropriate 'female' activities. This results in not only different attitudes towards various subjects, but also very different attitudes to different ways of organising work within a given subject, particularly as relates to talk or interactive activities.

Discussion methods are a good example of the sort of activity generally devalued among boys. There are other reasons why boys may find discussion difficult which relate to the ways they are less able to behave supportively towards each other. The degree of their competitiveness, inability to listen to one another, and lack of skill at verbal interaction (confined to a fundamental devaluing of discussion as a worthwhile process) can make it extremely difficult to have productive class discussions. Having said so, however, it is important to point

out that this is very much affected by what sort of discussion is being set up. In classes where discussion is used regularly as a valued and established activity, boys may participate enthusiastically. Discussions about sharing personal experience sometimes seemed to result in boys talking in extremely generalised or stereotyped terms, not listening to each other and complaining that they were wasting time. Interestingly, this was not the case in the first weeks after transferring from primary school. But the school setting soon 'taught' them not to 'open up' in front of classmates.

As already discussed these observations also relate to collaborative tasks. Boys often do not communicate sufficiently to plan or organise what they intend to do, and may end up each doing his own separate work, or else with one boy taking total responsibility while the others opt out completely.

As we will argue in the next chapter, school itself fosters an individualistic and competitive approach to learning, with children being measured and assessed against each other. These are characteristics regarded as 'typically' 'male' (while supportive, co-operative behaviour is 'typically' 'female', as women take the 'caring' supportive role in society). From our observations, it does seem that many boys and girls are set on to these paths, and do develop along these lines. A co-operative approach to collaborative activities is often fairly alien to many boys.

Notes

1   We made a search of the *British Humanities Index, British Education Index, London Bibliography of the Social Sciences, Register of the Educational Research in the UK., Index to Theses* (Universities of Great Britain and Northern Ireland), and the *Journal of Educational Research* (USA), and could not find anything about bullying and violence among boys at school or about social interaction among boys.

CHAPTER 3

Sexism in the School Structure and Organisation

So far we have discussed ways in which boys' behaviour in school may be problematic. However, we now go on to argue that in exploring the roots of the problem we must not only focus on the boys themselves but on the structure and organisation of the school system. We have become increasingly aware that there are almost infinite layers and levels which have to be considered if strategies adopted in the classroom with boys are to be more than merely cosmetic. Segregated boys' schools are one mechanism by which sex roles are reinforced. This is not to say that we think that boys' schools are more 'sexist' institutions, but that since they are predominantly all-male institutions, the sexism in them is very overt. The same structures and organisation will also perpetuate sexual divisions in mixed and girls' schools, but perhaps not be so easily recognisable. In our view the study of boys' schools provides an important model for the analysis of sexism in all schools.

In our society institutions are organised in such a way that power and success are derived from competitive, divisive and hierarchical structures. The only way we can achieve power and success within society (unless we are born in a rich or powerful position) is to conform to the rules of the institution. The continued dominance of some groups in society is dependent on their internalising and perpetuating establishment values. The result of this association between 'success' in a patriarchal capitalist system and those who hold the power in it is the identification of the system's characteristics with 'male' characteristics: such behaviour as competitiveness, aggressive-

ness and ambitiousness are seen as 'masculine' behaviours. Schools, as social institutions, are established as 'masculine' structures in which boys and girls need to operate in 'masculine' terms in order to succeed. This is particularly evident in all-boys' schools, where the expression of 'masculine' structures may be exaggerated.

In our report (Askew and Ross 1984) of work in one boys' school we tentatively suggested a direct association between the school organisation, policies on discipline and teaching methods, and the gender behaviour and relations we observed: 'We believe that boys' schools are usually built on values of competition, strength and power; bullying and "running down" become norms of gaining status'. This belief has been reinforced by our subsequent work in other boys' schools. Other research has made similar associations. Davison (1985) writes about being struck by what he considers the 'charged, hard-edged nature of life in a boys' school'. He argues that: 'The many elements that comprise the ethos of the school can perpetuate and, indeed, create the aggression a school seeks to control'. He states that there is a clear need for research in boys' schools into such things as the forms and manner of discipline; teaching styles; teacher expectations of pupil behaviour and the organisational structure of the school. The rest of this chapter is concerned with our research into these issues.

Discipline and authority in boys' schools

Discipline in boys' schools is often characterized by authoritarian power and control through strength. Whether or not male teachers actually use violence against pupils (and we have known cases where they have), boys we interviewed revealed that they *think* that violence will be used against them if they step out of line with a male teacher.

> John: I'm dead sure that if we acted up with Mr.—— he'd clobber us.
> Luke: He tells us he'll string us up against the wall if we don't shut up!

While such threats may be made with little intention of enforcement, nevertheless they encourage and reinforce the idea that discipline can only be attained and maintained by the 'strong' male teacher! Such attitudes make the discipline difficult for non-authoritarian teachers.

Teachers have discussed ways in which the aggression among boys is a reflection of the authoritarian structures within the school. For example, a male Head of Year in a boys' school which has made considerable strides towards analysing the issues and developing strategies to deal with them, reports to us in an interview:

> I think that bullying is often an acting out of the power structures of the school itself rather than the fault of individual boys. This discussion has come up very often in the last couple of weeks where we've been talking about the fact that, although we're shifting now, it has very much been a male structure and it might be more useful to look at a responsibility structure. The whole way of relating to boys in this school seems to come from a punitive approach and a blaming approach. There's a deficiency model and it's very aggressive. So you can imagine someone, kind of ticking along saying: 'Don't you dare bully this boy' and it's a kind of contradiction in terms where the actual process is in direct conflict with what's actually being said. I think one of the most important things is for people to become aware of how they deal with an issue like bullying. So it's not just a curricular thing, it's a school structure as well. Women are notable by their absence within our hierarchical structures so, although it's male-orientated, aggressive style if you like and a dominant style of dealing with someone who's gone against the rules or their behaviour is deficient in some way, the message is: 'This is how you get what you want', and I think they go: 'Ah ha', you know, 'This is the way'. So there's a modelling thing going on as well and it's very much a male modelling thing.
>
> I think there's probably a whole ethos where there's bullying as a way of going on. So I can see that bullying is, apart from obvious specific issues, a thread running through the way boys relate to one another. They see it as a competitive thing rather than a collaborative thing. That's how you establish yourself.

Another teacher talked to us about how he believes the means of controlling the boys within the structure of his school set up destructive power relationships:

> People don't have to feel it's a control issue and a power issue. I'm not saying that you don't need certain dynamics going on in

the classroom in order for people to pay attention, take information in. I think that's essential. It's a case of how that particular classroom climate comes about and whether you're there to educate or control, and the sorts of methods by which control is achieved seem to me too often to rely on an aggressive style and a controlling style. I think you can see a shift in our school to sharing the power with the class so that they engage much more in their own learning. A negotiated position that has real meaning for them means that you don't fall into the power thing again afterwards or they see the negotiation as a totally empty gesture. I think this power model is fundamentally a male model. I base this on my observation of how men behave. Also because it's by and large men who inhabit those regions. Also, for women to get into that structure they have to play out the man's game. It's sort of in order to establish credibility or some kind of equality in the situation they feel they need to be seen in those positions of power. I feel it's more useful to question the structure than to get into what's already there. I think it is a male structure because I think women are much more ready to be supportive to one another. I don't know why. It might be that the factor of oppression *caused* women to be more supportive because they had to. I think it's a much more useful way of working. I don't think men have that ability as much.

Apart from the maintenance of discipline and authority in boys' schools by actual and threatened physical punishment, there are other ways in which boys are kept 'in check' which also rely on power and strength, for instance, loud shouting at the boys to 'shut up'. When a boy *has* misbehaved it is usually dealt with in an individual and 'crisis-orientated' way. The individual boy is sent to see the (usually) male Head of House, Year or Department. Undisciplined behaviour is most usually an outcome of social relationships and is quite often something which involves *all* the boys in a class, not just one. For instance, it is fairly accepted that when the one pupil who is the 'bane' of the teacher's life ('if only he wasn't there the teaching would be easy') is removed, another invariably takes his place. There is constant peer-group pressure on individual boys to take the role of the joker or the class bully, or the disruptive pupil. The only way, we feel, to deal with this is to make bad behaviour in the class a subject for discussion. The Head of House who comes into the classroom to reprimand the class and warn them, is reinforcing the idea that the responsibility for behaviour lies solely with the teacher who is big enough and loud enough to enforce it. This attitude denies the possibility of pupils being self-disciplined or being able to co-operate for their own self-interest and out of consideration for others. Our evidence suggests that instead it is based on fear and power of the big over the small, the man over the boy and the adult over the child. It perpetuates the notion that pupils behave better with 'tough' and 'strict' teachers and undermines teachers who prefer not to rely on these methods of discipline. We have frequently heard some men and women teachers described as 'too soft'. Implicit in this description is the idea that the 'soft' teacher is a *bad* teacher.

The fact that the 'hard' teacher is setting impossible (even undesirable) norms and expectations is never raised. Although negotiated methods of discipline and authority *can* work within a school where norms are different, an incredible amount of work is needed to reach that point and often the strengths of 'soft' teachers go unrecognised. For instance, one of the hardest-working, creative and 'soft' teachers in a particular school, who did not work in an authoritarian way, was congratulated not on her hard work and skill but on her *luck* in having such a nice class of boys. These kinds of assumption, too, affect the ways in which some teachers respond to complaints about bad behaviour: 'He's not like that with me' suggests that the teacher is at *fault*, rather than that bad behaviour is unacceptable *whoever* the teacher.

In addition, there may be other consequences of discipline gained through aggressive methods. O'Hagan and Edmunds (1982) interviewed pupils to find their response to the different ways in which teachers respond to disruptive behaviour. They interviewed sixty girls and sixty boys aged thirteen and fourteen years. The result of the research showed that aggressive teaching strategies, which may appear initially to be effective in controlling misbehaviour, could well have deleterious consequences in other ways — such as the increased likelihood of truancy.

The pastoral system

The pastoral system in boys' schools is clearly directly related to discipline structures within the school. It usually takes the form of a House system rather than a year system. This means that some pupils in each year of the school belong to the same 'House'. Although in theory there are advantages to the system (such as boys getting a sense of and feeling part of the whole school, breaking down boundaries between peer-groups, allowing house tutors to get to know whole families) in practice it is often rooted in competition — one 'House' against the other. The following is typical of comments made to us: 'There's no kind of pastoral programme in my school. It's thought this would take time away from more important things. Pastoral care is simply seen in terms of dealing with individual "problems" '. Teachers in boy's schools have complained to us that the pastoral system in their schools is more concerned with the social control of boys rather than with developing an overview of pupils' achievement and progress or social well-being. Much of what seems to go under the heading of 'pastoral care' therefore appears to be somewhat negative. Pastoral care is identified in some boys' schools with 'problems', for example, truancy and bad behaviour. The positive aspects are very often lost: for example, ensuring a point of continued personal contact, offering guidance on personal or educational issues, or career development. This has contributed to a split between the academic and the pastoral. In many of the schools in which we have worked, if discipline deteriorated it was the responsibility of the Head of House (pastoral) rather than the Head of Department (academic). This invested certain members of staff with an aura of power in the eyes of the pupils. Why not share that responsibility by sending for the teacher next door or form tutor?

The social control element of the pastoral care system also results in and perhaps intensifies the 'labelling' process which occurs in schools. Because pupils tend to remain in the same house, with the same Head of House from the first to the fifth year, once they are labelled 'disruptive' they cannot easily lose that label. If the responsibility for discipline problems were spread more widely this might not happen so readily.

Competition

Most learning in schools, as we have observed, is based on competition. Children learn very early to see themselves as better or worse at writing, reading, running, drawing, than other children. The measure is how well they compare with every one else, not whether they are making progress. This approach to learning is reinforced by systems of stars, marks, tests and teachers comparing pupils. The examination system is a competitive system, with marks graded so that only a certain percentage can attain high grades each year. In all these ways, boys' schools are similar to other schools.

However, we feel that in boys' schools this competitiveness is more overt. In this society a high value is placed on competitiveness and it has become one of the stereotypical traits associated with masculinity. In mixed or girls' schools the competitiveness at the basis of all education in the system has been blurred, due to the presence of girls and a larger number of female staff. This is not to say that women and girls are not competitive or that competition isn't inherent in mixed and girls' schools. The point is the manifestation of competition will be less extreme and therefore less visible. Whether or not to encourage competition in girls has become a controversial issue. Some argue that we are all 'naturally' competitive and point to the way in which even small children boast 'I'm better than you, na na na-na na'. (However, it seems to us hardly surprising that this should be so given the kinds of comparisons which adults make so frequently.) Other people argue that, given the system as it is, the best we can do is instil in our pupils as great a competitive spirit as possible so that they will struggle more determinedly for success. This view sometimes concurs with calls for fewer 'progressive' teaching methods, and perhaps even a feeling that the 'good old days' of selection and grammar school education should be brought back. Given the lack of power which most of us feel in terms of actually changing the present system, it is tempting to opt for this view. One teacher put the dilemma as follows:

> It comes right down to what school is about. Some people argue that school has to reflect how society is, so after all it is a

competitive world and if kids are going to fit into it you have to make them competitive. Or whether schools can be an agent of change and it doesn't have to be dog eat dog.

Whether or not schools can be agents of change, we think that a competitive ethos does not aid learning. We think that more is likely to be learned *and* remembered if pupils work in a way which motivates and engages them in classroom activities. Reducing stress levels and improving social relationships is also particularly important.

Hierarchies in school

In the thirty or so boys' schools that we have visited, we have found it rare for women to be in senior management positions. Women are in the minority. Where women have posts of responsibility they tend to be in the humanities, languages or special needs departments. Decision-making in boys' schools tends to reflect the male authoritarian make-up of the school. There may on the surface appear to be a democratic decision-making structure. For example, we observed staff meetings where all staff were invited to 'air' their opinions. However, these meetings were often run on hierarchical lines, with the Head or senior management in the chair, and members of staff sitting in rows listening. One male member of staff talked to us about the problem of a hierarchical structure as follows:

> There seems to be a really deep kind of hierarchical structure and it seems to be that, in order to be successful, you have to rise up through the ranks and each stage you go up you seem to be removed further from colleagues down there somewhere. There's a kind of psychological distance, and to me it seems like a communication distance as well. The power seems to be in terms of you can tell people what to do — you have this duty. I think, because of the psychological distance, it doesn't allow for any support to go on. I don't think that people, therefore, can feel any ownership in their work situation and it's very stressful or potentially very stressful. I think when people are involved and engaged their motivation is there. And also, if there is a consultative structure or a very flat hierachy, then it's possible to

set up situations where people are able to consult perhaps in smaller groups and still have the links between the groups. It's possible for people to relate on a much more equal footing, and I think you make much better use of expertise. I think if people are experiencing difficulty or are feeling dissatisfied with anything that's going on, then rather than perhaps store it inside or resent their job or feel angry with other people, it can be aired. Or, if people need support or are having a terrible time — you know, it's OK to be vulnerable. The other model suggests that any sign of vulnerability is not fitting with this model, which, I think, is essentially a male model. The responsibility model is a support model. You may have responsibility for a particular area of work, but you have a more humane thread running through it.

In terms of the way in which pupils view teachers, there is a need to combat hierarchism. It may convey strong messages about who is to be granted respect in the institution and ideas about inferiority and superiority in relation to gender, race and class. Ways in which that power could be more equally shared include involving junior colleagues in decisions on discipline. Senior colleagues asking junior colleagues' opinions both in meetings and in front of pupils, junior colleagues being seen in a position where they are expert, knowledgeable or have particular skills outside their own classroom situation, for example, by taking assemblies.

The 'male' curriculum

The curriculum in boys' schools may also reinforce traditional male roles. We observed a heavy emphasis on competitive sport and on traditional 'male' subjects such as design and technology and science, while traditionally 'female' subjects such as home economics and child development were not on offer. Within the subjects, study centres on white male achievement in a predominantly Eurocentric way, for example, in science and in history. We also saw in the sixth form little provision for the arts and humanities. Many materials and resources used as part of these courses had a racist/sexist and class bias. For example, positive images of black girls and boys and of white girls were absent; in history, the struggles and resistance of black people were often invisible, as was the contribution made by women of all ethnic groups to historical developments. In school libraries the books on the shelves also reflected this bias. In our experience boys' schools are no worse than mixed or girls' schools in relation to this, and many individual teachers in these schools are struggling to make changes and write their own materials. But in boys' schools many teachers we spoke to do not see the point of addressing gender issues. For example, one teacher said: 'Why bother so much about whether or not there are pictures of girls when it doesn't matter so much because there aren't any here?' In our view, it is important to present positive images to girls with which they can identify, but also to present to boys alternatives to the predominantly white, middle-class, male view of the world. In any consideration of the curriculum questions sl.ould be asked about *who* controls what knowledge should be made available to children..

Attitudes towards boys as a reflection of the school ethos

We have argued that 'strength' plays an important part in the control of boys in schools. It is not surprising, therefore, that there tends to be a fairly uncritical view within the schools towards some forms of boys' aggressive behaviour. For example, frequent comments such as 'Boys will be boys' or 'That's just like a boy' are made with reference to aggressive behaviour by boys to each other. Indeed, the expectations that boys will be aggressive towards each other are often reflected in some teachers' beliefs about boys. Comments such as 'He's a cissy', or 'He's got to learn to take it like a man', carry implicit assumptions about 'normal' behaviour in boys. In our experience, a pervasive 'masculine' ethos is inherent in boys' schools — a kind of 'all boys together' feeling which reflects uncritically aggressive 'male' stereotypes. A woman teacher commented to us:

> Many of the men like and care about the kids very much. But they often show it by fighting! It's joke fighting of course, and both the boys and the men think it a lot of fun, but women would rarely relate to the boys like that.

This relates to what Davison (1985) has called 'the common culture of maleness': 'Male teachers in an all-boys classroom have access to this shared culture from which female teachers are debarred'. Margaret Sandra (1982) also found that 'all boys' or 'all girls' situations 'engender a particular atmosphere which has sufficient degree or consensus that conflict between pupils and pupils and teachers ... is much reduced and disruptive behaviour is confined'. This may reinforce the particular expectations of boys and girls in this society and perpetuate sexist assumptions.

The very reasons why some parents have stated they sent their sons to boys' schools are to do with this 'masculine' ethos. The following comments were made to us by parents we talked to: 'He's a bit "soft". I thought coming here would toughen him up. He's got to learn to stand up for himself'. 'I've sent my boy here because I want him to have more discipline. I like the fact that there's a cadet corps here'.

Teaching styles and school values

We have suggested that certain activities and teaching methods reflect 'norms' and values of the school (which we asserted are 'male' qualities and values) and thereby reinforce stereotypical 'masculine' behaviour in the boys. We also implied that this might explain the resistance and difficulty that many boys display when confronted with collaborative work, or non-product-orientated activities.

From primary school, activities are credited with being either 'work' or 'play' — 'If you do your maths and writing work you may do art work or look at books during your free time'. Notions of 'real work' and 'non-work' are clearly built into school life, and schools tend to value activities with visible end-products over activities with none. This is true also in general societal terms. 'What did you do today?' 'Nothing. I just visited a friend!', or 'I just read; I didn't do anything'. Generally speaking, what is valued in society (and school) relates to the stereotypical 'male role' of 'make' and 'do'. Interactive activities which relate to the 'female role' of social intercourse (and generally do not result in an end product) are not afforded the same status or recognised as 'real' or worthwhile activities, and are devalued accordingly.

While all school children work within this value system and will internalise it to some extent, our evidence shows that boys are more likely to do it to a far greater extent. In our view this is because it reflects and reinforces the qualities considered 'male' which boys have learned not only to develop in themselves, but to define the boundaries of behaviour. In this way, certain activities may be seen as a 'threat' to their masculinity.

Authoritarian teaching styles, where teachers place themselves in a dominant role in terms of both knowledge and control of behaviour, tend to reinforce power structures of 'weak' and 'strong', as well as 'right' and 'wrong' (in the sense of what is valuable to know). We feel this results in yet another way that status is achieved in terms of a power relationship. This is not to say that teachers should relinquish their role of creating a structure in which pupils can feel safe and secure and know what is expected of them.

Some teachers, we observed, worked towards maintaining class discipline through alternative methods, drawing their status from mutual respect established within the classroom. Methods they used included attempting to develop genuine relationships with the boys; helping the boys talk about their behaviour; breaking down the 'macho' approach to discipline; helping to develop collective responsibility as opposed to individual responsibility as a way of working toward collaboration rather than competition; and generally helping to develop pupil autonomy through facilitation and guidance; working towards developing a supportive atmosphere where boys no longer feel under as much pressure to 'take it like a man'. Two important results of adopting alternative teaching styles might be to provide a model and validation of behaviour and interaction which does not rely on power and strength.

We have argued that the value system implicit in schools will reflect that of the white, middle-class male value system in wider society. It follows that the status and value ascribed to teachers will reflect this to some extent. It may be, therefore, that any teacher who is not white, male or middle-class starts from a position of automatic disadvantage in many respects. Boys clearly seem to have different expectations of their male and female teachers. They expect dominant, authoritarian behaviour from some male teachers (at least initially). Not only do boys expect male teachers to be authoritarian figures but, when they are, it confirms boys' expectations and provides a role model of masculinity in terms of superior power or strength. The boys' deference to these male teachers is in terms of power relationships rather than drawing respect from other criteria. There are various important ways that men and women teachers occupy different social positions within the classroom, and we discuss these in the next chapter.

CHAPTER 4

Women Teachers' Experiences

Women teaching in boys' schools often find themselves in a particularly difficult position. Although women's individual social position, circumstances, backgrounds and attitudes may vary considerably, we noted certain common experiences. These related to the ways women teachers are perceived, undermined and sexually harassed. The issues we shall discuss in this chapter have been raised by women teachers while working within schools, in schools' women's groups, in workshop situations and at several conferences (both mixed and women only).

A recent ILEA Report (1985) stated that the main difficulties women face in boys' schools are: isolation, sexual harassment and an undervaluing of their contribution to school responsibilities. Among problems mentioned were hostility of male staff and discrimination by management and governors over appointments, including direct discrimination at the short-listing stage, unacceptable questions being asked at interviews, and general pressure or intimidation to prevent women seeking promotion. The extent of such incidents has led us to focus on the common context of women's experience in school, and to ask questions about its essential nature. The pattern which emerged clearly indicated that these difficulties and observations occurred directly in relation to institutional elements.

This, for us and for many women teachers, has been a crucial recognition. It has meant that, instead of identifying ourselves as failing or deficient, we now are beginning to examine what it

55

is about the school as an institution that creates these situations. Being able to locate the source of our difficulties in the structure and organisation of the school itself begins to give us some defence against the way schools usually locate the problems in us, the women teachers (for example, 'not being able to cope', being 'too soft'). By sharing our experiences in the school situation we can effectively identify the underlying sexism of the institution.

Some of the comments that women make in this chapter are specific to boys' schools. However, the issues we look at will be useful to those interested in exploring the more subtle forces at work within mixed schools which affect women's position, roles and status.

Teaching styles and boys' attitudes

As we argued in the last chapter, women are at an automatic disadvantage in schools run on authoritarian lines. When a school is run on the basis of 'authority equals strength and power' and discipline is seen in terms of control, women may find it extremely difficult to operate. When there is this sort of prevailing 'macho' atmosphere in the school, there is intense pressure for teachers to adopt authoritarian teaching styles or be seen as incompetent. Many women can find they are unable to work along these lines. They have described how they feel that whatever alternative strategies they try they are inevitably understood in terms of the 'norms' of the school. Women teachers who attempt to establish discipline through developing relationships with pupils and reasoning with them, rather than dictating to them, will probably be seen as 'soft' teachers who are taken less seriously than 'hard' teachers. One woman described this to us as follows: 'I hate the way that bullying passes for teaching and discipline in lessons and in the corridors. It makes my way of working with pupils seem weak to them'. This is not to imply that all women are unable or unwilling to work in authoritarian ways. But there are various reasons why women teachers may not wish to, or might find it difficult. Often it can simply be a matter of smaller stature and a higher voice that makes authority through physical (or vocal) threat difficult. There is also the expectation that women, just because they are women, will take on a 'mothering' role. 'Women teachers are more understanding', a male pupil told us. 'I suppose a lot of women can adopt a much more friendly, caring approach', a male teacher said. In an authoritarian institution, measures of success are inextricably bound up with 'good discipline'. A good teacher is seen as one who can 'control' the class. As one woman teacher explained: 'It doesn't matter what I try to do in my lessons, or how creatively or conscientiously I prepare them — most male colleagues see me as a "useless" teacher because my lessons are noisy'.

In this atmosphere, many women have described to us the necessity to abandon teaching styles based on equality and mutual respect, and attempt (however unsuccessfully) to conform to the norms of the system:

> I feel when I teach boys I have to be much more authoritarian and aggressive than I want to be, otherwise they take absolutely no notice.

> I have had to prove myself as a strict, tough teacher ... but there are still some boys who don't rate me at all as an authority — and sometimes they'll laugh at me.

> Authority in my school is in terms of bullying or intimidation. Some women yell wildly because they can't use muscle mass as a threat or are so frustrated. I personally have little problem since I teach small groups in a team situation with a woman Head of Department who has learned to threaten like the men.

> I feel in a dilemma as a woman teacher. Whatever I do, I feel I end up reinforcing the norms of how teachers should behave in a boys' school ... By adopting a more authoritarian style, I feel I'm validating this way of teaching and invalidating alternative methods. Yet if I take a more creative approach, I'm 'acting like a woman'.

Clearly, not all men are able or even want to teach in heavy-handed authoritarian ways. Some will face their own version of disciplinary problems or ridicule for failing to conform to stereotyped expectations. None the less, because the threat of physical power is central to an authoritarian structure many men teachers need not overtly express their physical authority — it is implicit in the ethos of the school itself. This compounds the situation, since it means that there will be some men who will be able to teach in less overtly authoritarian ways without 'discipline problems'. Therefore, it appears that it is the incompetence of women that causes their own problems with pupil control, rather than anything about the school itself. The fact is that generally men, by virtue of being men, are backed up by the system, while women are undermined by it.

This may seem to lead to a conclusion that women have no place teaching boys, particularly in a boys' school. But there is more involved than the ability to maintain control. The ways that women suffer or have difficulty within an authoritarian system highlight the norms of that system. The implications for the ways boys will develop and the values they will hold within a system that equates physical power with strength and 'might with right' are very frightening. Some of its effects are evident in women teachers' experience of boys' attitudes towards them. These observations clearly underline the values and behaviour that the boys are being taught by the school to validate and emulate. These women teachers made the following comments to us:

> Some boys in my class are always doing things that are intended to demonstrate that I have no power over them. Often it's very subtle — maybe just the way they look at me or their tone of voice. Of course, sometimes, it's very out-front and unbelievably rude, sexist comments, answering back or direct challenges.

> Several boys in the class have told me I should try to 'teach more like a man'.

> Boys have told me outright that they would never behave in a man teacher's class the way they do in mine.

> My experience of teaching boys is that the style of presentation must always be tough and no-nonsense or they disregard it. You must always be 100% on top of activities involving things like video operation or they delight that you don't understand equipment.

> In a boys' school, because of the lack of girls, the boys tend to notice the female staff and they often make unpleasant remarks and speak of them in a sexist way. Mind you, in a mixed school I guess the girls get it.

Boys we talked to said of their women teachers in interviews: 'She should act more like a man teacher', or 'She's a soft woman teacher'. Some women said they adopt more authoritarian methods simply to survive: 'I feel when I teach boys I have to be much more authoritarian and aggressive than I want to be, otherwise they take absolutely no notice'. And another woman: 'As a woman teacher in an all-boys school I feel almost "invisible" sometimes. I think there is a male culture in the classroom that I can never enter into'.

Michelle Stanworth (1981) found that: 'Both boys and girls feel more at ease, more attentive and more able to participate in classroom activity when they are taught by teachers of their own sex'. When one of us first began teaching in an all-boys school she was struck by the initial lack of friendliness from the boys. Early on, she heard one boy greet a woman teacher in a friendly way when he passed her in the playground: Another boy, overhearing, said to him: 'You big poof'. In her experience of teaching in mixed schools there didn't seem to be this pressure on boys not to be friendly to women teachers. Boys' schools, on the whole, do not seem to encourage close, non-aggressive friendly relations between either the boys themselves or the boys and staff. Jon Davison (1985) investigated boys' attitudes to women teachers. He says that a typical comment from a fourth-year boy was:

> At an all-boys school, boys are more liable to respect a male teacher than a female one. The female teacher would be more vulnerable to mickey-taking, lip and cheek. Whereas if a man was teaching, the boys might think twice.

Other remarks he mentions included: 'Women have to put up with abuse, dirty remarks'. 'You get away with murder with women teachers'. 'When men teachers shout, you shut up. When women shout you take no notice'. 'Women ain't strict ... they're fools'. Such remarks, in our opinion, reflect the overall position of women in the school and the general structure of power and control and attitudes to discipline cited in the previous chapter.

Carabis and Dodds (1984) also found that boys behave differently towards women teachers — that boys 'tried it on more'. They summed up boys' behaviour as including, in addition to explicit sexual harassment, looks, body language, verbal abuse and demeaning attitudes towards women.

They suggest that language can include a judgement of women based on their sexuality rather than ability to do the job.

Evidently most boys respect women teachers less than men as teachers and believe they learn more from men teachers. They often like and feel liked more by women, find them more understanding and their lessons more interesting and enjoyable. For example, a boy has said to us:

> You learn more in Mr ——'s class and Mr ——'s class because they really know how to control us. Lots of the women are a bit 'soft'. But you can talk to some of them. I like Ms ——'s class because it's the most interesting.

This quote indicates a confusion of values in the boys in that the qualities that bring them more warmth, understanding and pleasures are not worthy of respect. The boys not only learn that 'hard' behaviour is appropriate 'male' behaviour and 'soft' caring behaviour is female; but also that 'hard' is superior to 'soft', so they develop a disdain for what they identify as female behaviour, to be deplored and avoided at all costs.

Women teachers undermined

The undermining of women teachers may occur out of the 'best intentions', but reflects the assumptions and attitudes about women held by some male staff members. Women have described being undermined or being 'rescued' by men in several ways, including the following:

> I find myself being undermined by male colleagues — sometimes when they think they are 'protecting' me. For example, there's a man who teaches in the room across from me. Whenever the noise level in my lessons reaches a certain point, he'll burst into the room to quieten down the class or tell them off. It makes me feel totally stripped of authority in front of the boys.

> I sent a boy to the Head of Department (a man) over an episode where he spoke to me with abusive language. The Head of Department told the boy he 'shouldn't talk like that in front of Miss ——' — meaning the issue was that he had sworn in front of a woman.

I found a degree of protectiveness from the mainly male staff towards the small number of women staff. Soon after I arrived there was an incident between a boy and myself ... It was observed from the staffroom window by a male teacher who wanted to punish the boy. I reported that the matter was solved as far as I was concerned, but my male colleague was very rejected at not being able to leap to my defence.

On one occasion, when teaching a very difficult class of fourth years, bottom stream, who had responded well to me and were very attentive, I was interrupted by a man entering my room and, without any introduction, threatening any boy with a beating who caused me bother.

The point about 'rescuing' (however 'well meant') is that it expresses a fundamental belief that women are essentially less competent or weaker or less able to cope than men, and conveys these messages to boys. In a mixed school it also conveys messages to girls who are, in a sense, being 'told' what it means to be a female. This kind of subtle sexism is invisible yet likely to be internalised by all, boys, girls, men and women. This kind of 'protective' attitude to some women teachers is a result of assumptions made by some men based on the kind of stereotypes about women discussed in Chapter 1. The result for women may be an internalisation of their 'inferiority' and feelings of powerlessness and not being able to cope.

The way in which male colleagues react towards their female colleagues will reflect the stereotypes about women in relation to gender, race, class and sexuality. For example, some women teachers may not be patronised in a 'protective' way, but in other ways which are equally or more damaging. Older women may also suffer from being patronised in ways that are not specifically protective but give the message that they are generally useless and ineffectual.

Often women teachers who are having trouble with discipline in the school are themselves seen as the 'problem'. For example, one experienced woman teacher who came on a weekend course we ran for women teachers who worked with boys, came because both she and her Head had presumed that the course would 'help me learn how to handle the boys'. Another woman told us that when she reported to her Head of Department that she felt she was having discipline problems because the boys were not taking her seriously as a woman teacher, his response was: 'How about spending a couple of lessons observing John — I'm sure you'll learn a lot from him'. John was a very big man with a loud voice who, needless to say, had very few problems with discipline. This kind of comment indicates that the women teachers are very often identified as the 'problem', rather than the disciplinary structures in the school. Both men and women teachers who either do not want to, or cannot, fit into this aggressive style are labelled as 'unable to cope'.

There is a category of undermining behaviour towards women from some men that, we believe, is directly misogynistic and fully intended. Although many men do not behave in this way to women, it none the less appears to occur, can be very damaging, and can also be very subtle. Women have described to us incidents with male staff which they believed were deliberately aimed at making them feel belittled or humiliated:

> I was sitting in the staffroom at 5 pm when a male staff member asked me: 'Haven't you got a home to go to and a husband to cook for?'

> I've heard from pupils that some male teachers make sexist or racist jokes and comments to pupils as a regular part of their lessons.

> Some boys in my form have repeated some of the 'jokes' their (male) C.D.T. teacher has told them. I have to say I was shocked. They were really disgusting — the usual sexist jokes about women.

> I was told by a male Inspector, after a request to retrain in C.D. & T., that I did not look right for the part and maybe Home Economics would be more my line; and 'Why don't you go home and talk to your husband about your career prospects?'

> I sent a note to a male science teacher with my form when they were going to his lesson, asking him if he could complete and return their reports. He read it and then said aloud, in a fury and in front of my whole form: 'I'm not having any bitch tell me what to do'.

> After I'd dealt with an incident between two boys, a male colleague came up, asked for an account of what happened, and what I'd done, and then told the boys they were lucky it wasn't

him who'd seen them first — the implication being that I was a push-over.

I get comments about the way I dress, sometimes with direct sexual innuendo, from some men on the staff — sometimes right in front of the boys, too.

I feel I am dismissed and invisible in all sorts of ways by several men on the staff. I have to sustain a personal determination not to be discounted, but I would prefer not to have to resort to such tactics.

I was told by a senior member of staff, after an absence of three days, 'If the climate does not suit you, girl, why don't you go back home?'

What's a little girl like you doing with such a big red apple? (said to a 50-year-old woman teacher).

I was shown a newspaper clipping 'French women are dirty, they only change their knickers once a week' — and then he said to me 'You're French, you ought to know'.

Women who complain about this kind of treatment tend not to be treated seriously. They are quite likely to become the 'joke' feminist. If they complain they are likely to be labelled as 'nag', 'aggressive' or 'one-track-minded'. The woman is seen as wrong and unnatural, not 'feminine'. The common use of the term 'girl' when applied to women teachers is in itself disrespectful and undermining. Such behaviour makes it difficult for women teachers to criticise some male colleagues for their attitudes and behaviour.

Many women have complained to us that their observations, particular incidents and general difficulties are often not taken seriously by some male colleagues. They are made to feel foolish, told they are being 'hysterical' or 'neurotic', or else (most commonly) that they 'don't have a sense of humour' or are 'taking it too seriously'. The message, once again, is that the problems lie within the women themselves, are not real issues, and are not important: 'Whenever I complain of a sexist incident, the general male reaction is "Here she goes again" '. 'I can't tell you how many times I've been told "don't be hysterical" by male staff. They act like I'm imagining the whole problem — or else that *I* am the problem'.

Staff meetings

Women teachers are often subjected to undermining attitudes and behaviour at staff meetings. Dissatisfaction is usually focused on the way meetings are organised, or the way contributions from women are dismissed as of no value:

> Staff meetings are mostly a monologue from the Head, with contributions from senior staff (all male).

> When I do make a point, there is silence for a minute, then they continue as though I hadn't said anything. But often later on a man will repeat the point I made, and then it will be taken up.

It is evident that the organisation of staff meetings directly affects the position of women attending them. There is an unspoken, implicit value system in any method of organisation. When the organisation is in terms of a hierarchical structure, we believe this carries 'encoded' messages about power, status and value. And, of course, there is also the issue of who, within such a context, is 'worth' listening to. It is a structure loaded with values ascribed by the dominant groups within it: anyone not part of the dominant culture is likely to be dismissed — in some sense excluded before they begin.

Sexual harassment

Most points raised in this section can be subsumed under the heading 'implicit sexual harassment'. We interpret the term in its broadest sense; that is, all the ways that women are negatively affected by their position of social subordination. In the male institution of a boys' school sexual harassment may be 'invisible' because it is so 'normal' within the establishment.

In its broadest sense, sexual harassment (although varying in context, manifestation and degree) is a constant feature of women's lives. It usually has, on some level, an implied threat of violence. We define sexual harassment as any behaviour, however subtle, that identifies or responds to women as less than equal to, or primarily existing for, men. It expresses itself in all the ways women are physically or verbally assaulted, undermined, excluded, denied power, made invisible, expected to defer, held down and generally 'kept in their place' both by individual men and by male institutions.

Benn (1985) writes about sexual harassment in terms of the construction of masculinity:-

> The description 'sexual harassment' itself rings wrong. To me it conjures up images of 'moments', episodes of coercion, bad times ... but there is also something overwhelmingly ordinary, tedious and day-to-day about it. The point is, isn't sexual harassment really about masculinity? But shouldn't any campaign against it contain some recognition of, and commitment to change, masculinity — rather than simply to amend 'unacceptable', 'individual' 'male behaviour'?

Male domination depends upon the subordination of women. 'Femininity' is developed in relation to 'masculinity'. In one sense, everything which expresses the subordination of women is an expression of masculinity. The term 'masculinity' has become synonymous with power, and especially power over women.

The implications of defining sexual harassment in this way are enormous in the context of school, and boys' schools in particular. Schools are, after all, based on power relationships, for example, who has knowledge and who doesn't, adult and child. Sexual harassment is, in a sense, an expression of masculinity and this suggests that in an institution that is organised in overtly 'masculine' terms, values and attitudes which promote the subjugation of women must be absolutely implicit in its very structure. We have suggested that in boys' schools the curriculum, discipline, teaching, methodology and most interactions are displays of masculinity. One of the ways that boys are learning to define their own masculinity and notions about women is by this example of 'masculinity' and masculine behaviour.

Pat Mahoney (1985) has shown how girls are continually sexually harassed in mixed schools. In boys' schools that harassment is directed at the women staff. Below are some examples of the kinds of harassment women have talked to us about. Some of it is physical, for example:

> Every time I turned my back on a first-year class of boys, one of

them touched my bum. When I turned around they sat 'innocently'. I felt completely humiliated. How could they take me seriously as a teacher when they were touching my bum?

Some of it is sexual innuendo: 'I went in to cover a class of fifth-year boys I didn't know. As I walked in one of them said, "I wouldn't come in here if I was you, you might get raped"'. 'Sometimes it's something said that is supposed to be a joke but it leaves me feeling sick inside'. Some of it is about physical appearance: 'A male colleague said to me: "I'll bet you don't have any trouble with the sixth form boys when you wear that!"' Some of it is written: 'I'm forever finding obscene graffiti in our text books'. 'I've had some absolutely disgusting notes from pupils. I felt so ashamed of one that I never told anyone about it'. Some of it is belittling:

> I find boys especially difficult if I take them after they've had a lesson with a man teacher who's particularly 'big' and 'strong' in his approach to the class. Somehow, this always results in the boys laughing at me and joking about me really a lot.

Some of it is verbal abuse: 'I've been called an "old bag", a "slag", and a "whore" by some first-year boys'. None of these examples are about extreme, overt, violent sexual harassment. This is not because we have not heard about this sort of episode — we know it to exist. However, as physical attacks may be the only form of sexual harassment officially recognised, we are focusing on descriptions of less acknowledged forms of abusive behaviour towards women.

One disturbing aspect of sexual harassment in schools is the attitudes towards it expressed by male pupils. Carabis and Dodds (1984) write about the results of their interviews with boys on this subject: 'Boys we interviewed expressed surprise that women should object to this treatment as they consider it natural'. 'Part of the problem is that what we believe is sexual harassment is regarded as "natural" male behaviour'. Indeed, we believe it is this 'normality' of sexual harassment, its acceptance by our society, especially in male establishments, that renders it invisible and unrecognised except for the most extreme cases. So, in most institutions, there are rarely satisfactory channels for complaint by women who have been sexually harassed. Few schools have established effective procedures for dealing with sexual abuse.

The idea that women 'exaggerate' the problem, or get 'too het up' about it, is clear from descriptions given to us about the way many men in the senior hierarchy deal with it. Women have said that they are often asked to 'prove' the incident in a way which would be quite unheard of if a male member of staff were to accuse a boy of hitting him. The implication is that women are not to be believed. This, of course, further undermines a woman teacher if she has been sexually harassed. One Head of a boys' school even said to a group of women who went to him to discuss incidents of harassment in the school: 'We didn't have any problems with sexual harassment in the school until the Women's Group was formed'. This Head saw the women's group as encouraging their 'neuroses' rather than as giving women confidence and an understanding that their situation was not unique.

Many of the behavioural problems women teachers face from boys in their classrooms are directly related to issues of sexual harassment. Women often have difficulty in asserting authority because of not being taken seriously as women. This extends to the attitude that it is a woman's own fault if she has been heckled or sexually harassed in some way — it is a sign of her own incompetence as a teacher. Most women are therefore unable to make sexual harassment public without putting themselves in a vulnerable and even more difficult position.

The version of masculinity rooted in power and control is dependent upon a view of women as wishing to be overpowered and creating circumstances where they will be controlled. It assumes everything women do is with men in mind and will be motivated in some way to gain or reject male attention. In this way, women are also blamed for the more overt forms of sexual harassment, both in school and in society at large.

As we have intimated, one of the greatest difficulties about all but the most brutal forms of sexual harassment is making it visible and having it taken seriously. It is rarely censured because most of it is considered an expression of 'normal', 'healthy' masculinity. It is often described as 'harmless', 'innocent', or 'natural'. We believe that because dominant groups in society generally presume to 'know' what subordinate groups are like and what they want, they are generally surprised and disbelieving if they are told anything else. They reject anything else as atypical. We have seen women who refuse to behave in the role assigned to them being labelled as, at best, unusual, or as 'frustrated', 'aggressive' or 'abnormal'.

We have also heard male teachers suggest that women themselves collude in their own sexual harassment. By this they appear to mean that a woman teacher's behaviour is sometimes flirtatious or her dress is attractive. We disagree with this argument for several reasons:

1 the removal of moral responsibility for the harassment from the perpetrator to the 'victim';

2 the suggestion that because someone looks 'nice' it is all right to be rude to them, or even to attack them;

3 the reinforcement of the idea that women are sexual objects and should be reacted to as such, rather than out of respect for them as teachers.

In our experience there are some men in senior management who have difficulty with the idea that women, rather than senior management, should be involved with dealing with incidents of sexual harassment. In one school we visited, however, the male senior management do not deal with incidents of sexual harassment directly. In cases of sexual harassment boys are suspended and their parents are invited to a meeting with a member of the senior management and the woman involved or her woman representative. Before the boy is allowed back into school he is 'counselled' by two women on the staff who explain why his behaviour has caused offence (if he doesn't know), and it is carefully explained what the consequences of his actions will be in case of future incidents of this nature.

Below are some ideas on dealing with sexual harassment which came out of a weekend conference we organised for women teachers:

1 There needs to be a structure for dealing with sexual harassment — a consistent approach to the problem.

2 Sexual harassment must be made recognisable and visible.

3 It needs to be easily apparent that women are in an official position to respond to and deal with sexual harassment.

4 Women must have the option to have cases of sexual harassment dealt with by women only.

5 Women dealing with cases of sexual harassment should not be asked to break confidentiality. To spread details of incidents is to compound sexual harassment.

6 Sexual harassment must be put on the agenda for discussion in schools. It needs to be clearly defined in order to make it clear what it is and that it is not the 'fault' of individual women or girls.

7 A record of incidents should be kept to monitor the scope of the problem.

8 Sexual harassment undermines the woman teacher's authority — it should be made clear that sexual harassment does not occur because she cannot control the class.

The Women's Groups within the school

In a number of boys' schools a women's group has been formed to respond to and combat sexism. This can give women the opportunity to share experiences, support each other, identify issues of sexism within the school, and thus politicise themselves and begin to devise strategies for change.

Women's groups have been perceived as threatening, faced overt or open hostility and have been attacked as 'sexist' because of their exclusion of men. The idea that women-only meetings are 'sexist' indicates the misunderstanding which many people have about the term. Sexism stems from prejudiced and discriminatory attitudes together with the *power* to act on these assumptions. To argue that it is 'sexist not to allow men into women's groups' is to ignore the fact that in education, as in other areas, women are both stereotyped as inferior in many ways *and* that the control of the institution rests, to a large extent, in the hands of men. There are strong arguments for Womens' Groups. People who join together in order to confront and combat their victimisation are not *creating* the problem — they are *responding* to it.

Women's groups have found it productive to set particular objectives at a practical level as well as operating as a support and consciousness raising group. For instance women have reported that their group works best when they have a clear focus or task in mind. The women in a women's group may have very differing political perspectives and needs, and therefore the uniting feature may be the fact that they all work together towards a particular goal. For example, women's groups have organised conferences on sexism for their male colleagues; organised new courses on particular aspects of the curriculum; produced 'anti-sexist' posters and other materials; produced policies on such issues as sexual harassment.

Each school situation is different, will have different 'immovable' forces and different potential for change. Women's groups have started by looking for 'chinks' in their own school situations where inroads would be made.

We include here a set of suggestions for the type of activity which may be undertaken in Women's Groups which was drawn up at a conference for Women Teachers.

- Trying to make some specific objectives.
- Trying to include all the women in the school, where possible, not only teachers.
- Initiating things in other groups (Don't isolate yourselves).
- Consciousness raising.
- Giving one another support.
- Dealing with sexual harassment.
- Looking at the position of women teachers in the school and making suggestions.
- Taking on the planning of an anti-sexist conference or whole school meeting, etc.
- Practising difficult situations.
- Dealing with hostilities toward the women's group.
- Dealing with divisions within the group.
- Looking at curricula imbalance and content, including resources.
- Producing documents and written statements.
- Fighting invisibility in school meetings.
- Looking at sexist issues in relation to race and class issues.
- Producing own resources.
- Thinking about ways of working with the union.
- Assertion training.

A list of general problems at school with sexist implications was also drawn up. The areas pin-pointed by the women at the conference underscored the kinds of issues raised in our own experience and research, and reflect many points we raise in this book. The list includes:

- Curriculum imbalance.
- Forming a women's group (also dealing with divisions within it and hostilities towards it).
- Sexual harassment.
- Numbers of women teachers within the school: scales, position in hierarchy.
- Women's lack of access to effective discussion; structure of staff meetings; other meetings.
- Pressures on pupils from stereotyping.
- Parental contact; helping parents find ways of stating their criticism; positive involvement.
- Disseminating and implementing anti-sexist initiatives:
  (a) in the classroom (or as a specific course).
  (b) at a whole school level.
  (c) in terms of individual efforts.
  (d) resistance to change from other staff members.
- Curriculum content, materials used, etc. (as existing).
- Discipline.
- Amount and use of pastoral time.

This chapter has concentrated on some sexist experiences women have described in school, and some ways they are responding to this generally. In the next chapter we go on to look at specific anti-sexist strategies with boys in the classroom.

CHAPTER 5

Strategies for Working with Boys

Much of this chapter and the opinions expressed in it are built on our experience in one boys' school over a period of two years teaching and monitoring a course specifically set up to tackle issues of sexism and provide equal curricular opportunities. During the last three years we have both continued to work alongside teachers in the classroom and to develop materials for anti-sexist work with boys tried out in a wide range of different schools. (We include some examples of these materials in the text.)

It has been argued that anti-sexist work in school must be 'girl-centred education' (Weiner 1985). We accept that it is girls who are directly oppressed by sexism in school, as in many other areas of their lives, and that it is true that most education in schools is already 'boy-centred' in the sense that it is the achievement and experience of men which forms the greater part of the curriculum content. Boys, as we showed in Chapter 2, have also been labelled a 'problem' in the classroom — in relation to being more demanding and disruptive and therefore negatively affecting girls' experience of education in the mixed classroom.

Many teachers, however, are also concerned about the problems for the boys themselves. As we have argued, while girls and women are exploited and oppressed by sexism, boys are under unnecessary pressure in school to conform to masculine stereotypes which result in damaging expectations from both teachers and other boys, and stereotyped views of girls being reinforced. As we have shown earlier, boys are taught to compete with one another, to struggle to prove themselves physically, and quite literally to fight for status. Some may argue that working with boys on these issues is not in itself 'anti-sexist'. Trefor Lloyd (1985), a youth trainer who has done much work with boys on issues of manhood, masculinity and sexism, writes that:

> Boys' work, as I see it, *is not* anti-sexist work. Its focus is clearly with boys' needs and any work that is anti-sexist must, in my view, be primarily focused on young women (as the main 'victims' of sexism). However, I believe the *effects* of boys' work *are* anti-sexist. In doing this work the results appear to be an undermining of the young men's institutional sexism. As the young men's awareness of themselves grows, their need to participate and support abuse and containment of young women reduces.

We do not want to make a distinction between actually doing work with the boys and the effects of any such work. We argue, in fact, that it is the *intentions* which matter, and we intend that our work with boys challenges oppression and therefore includes an anti-sexist dimension.

We argued in the introduction to this book that for any school to tackle issues of power and inequality requires a fundamental reorganisation of the whole curriculum in terms of both the content and teaching methods (particularly with reference to which knowledge it is thought necessary to transmit). Such fundamental rethinking would have to be within the framework of challenging dominant and ethnocentric forms of knowledge. Such a new curriculum would be anti-sexist, as well as anti-racist and anti-classist, and equally accessible to *all* pupils. Change can happen at various levels. It can involve these kinds of fundamental change which challenge sexism at a structural level within the institution, or it can involve exploring attitudes and assumptions of teachers and pupils. This chapter describes work of the latter kind done with boys. We feel this is an important part of all pupils' education as it gives them awareness and understanding of sexist issues while, at the same time, offering them some strategies for coping. However, we recognise that the pupils themselves are not in a position to change the nature of oppression, whether in or out of school, and in different ways and to different degrees, are victims of it.

While girls are the chief victims of sexual oppression and therefore more resources need to be allocated to meeting the particular problems for girls, boys also need 'anti-sexist' education as a way of both undermining the brutalising effects of the construction of masculinity in this society and, by implication, challenging the effects of male sexism on girls. Most of our experience of anti-sexist work with boys has either been in setting up special courses to this end, or in developing 'topics' or units on particular issues of sexism within existing subjects.

Specific 'anti-sexist' courses for boys

Courses have been set up, both in boys' and mixed schools to focus especially on sexism and equal opportunities for boys. In mixed schools separate-sex work has been undertaken mainly in the pastoral curriculum. Because the socialisation processes for girls and boys are so different, as are our images of ourselves and our experiences, explicit anti-sexist courses for girls and boys also have to be very different. Explicit anti-sexist courses for girls have focused on sharing experiences of sexism, making its patterns visible, and equipping them with positive ways of offsetting it. With boys, teachers have worked on areas such as domestic role imbalances; unequal access to job opportunities; and stereotypes in the media and in books. Discussion around the more fundamental gender issues as they affect boys has been built into some anti-sexist courses — exploring with boys the kinds of pressure they are under, for instance, to act tough and not to show or talk about their feelings. The ways in which boys relate to one another have been addressed using themes like 'friendship' or 'bullying'. The aim has been to create a supportive classroom atmosphere which will encourage stereotyped 'norms' of masculinity to be challenged.

There are few such courses for boys in existence, and these often have a twofold approach which includes both the intention of fighting sexism and also offering boys access to those areas of the curriculum which have traditionally been viewed as 'female' areas. The course we were originally involved in developing had the following aims. First, to provide equal curriculum opportunities (including childcare studies and domestic crafts) to help boys to learn to take domestic responsibility and not to regard this as a women's realm. Second, to combat sexism by:

1 Helping boys to learn to express themselves and relate to others in ways traditionally considered to be within the female realm and not masculine attributes; developing behaviour which is often repressed in boys and men (this includes communicating in intimate ways; co-operation rather than competition; being supportive to each other; feeling responsible for the emotional well-being of each other).
2 Exploring explicit gender issues. In this context the following aims will be worked towards:
    (i) an examination of male and female stereotypical roles, attitudes and values;
    (ii) an awareness of the ways in which sex-role stereotyping imposes limits on the behaviour of both men/boys and women/girls;
    (iii) an exploration of positive alternatives to sex-role stereotypical behaviour.

We have found that provision of equal curricular opportunities, though very important in itself, does not automatically challenge sexist attitudes and behaviour in schools. Learning to cook, or learning about children, does not necessarily change boys' stereotyped notions about roles in the home. We have often heard comments such as: 'It's useful for when my wife goes into hospital' or 'It's a good idea because I might be on my own for a while before I get married'. In certain schools 'equal opportunities' work has been used as a foil for tackling some of the fundamental issues. For example, boys worked together in a small group making a meal and then eating it (often with a guest), as an opportunity to develop their ability to work collaboratively as well as develop a sense of responsibility for another person's well-being. The assessment built into the work allowed the boys to reflect, not on how good their finished food was but on how well they have worked together. The making and eating of a meal together in groups provided a valuable opportunity to develop social skills. We have often used practical work as a means of enabling discussion and thought about the topic rather than as an end in itself. For example, we used toy-making and book-making to allow the boys to think about the needs of young children and sex-role stereotyping.

Work on early childhood is incorporated into several 'anti-sexist' courses in boys' schools. The aims of this work have included: to extend equal opportunities by offering boys the chance to learn about young children; to encourage boys to regard child-care as the concern of males as well as females; to challenge role-stereotyped images of men and women; to examine how children are socialised into gender stereotypes; and to help boys to share their experiences and relate on a more personal level.

In two schools where we have worked, the boys had an additional sense of purpose when working on a child-development course by organising their own visits to the infant or nursery class of their old primary school. These visits were very successful and resulted, in some cases, in the boys being invited back to do such things as cooking with younger children or helping with teaching English as a second language.

We found it useful, when encouraging boys to share their own experiences, to relate our own memories of childhood and wrote stories to this end.

We have found that it was often less threatening to examine how younger children are socialised into gender stereotypes. For example, we discussed the toys we had played with and books we had read as young children (see Figures 1 and 2 — we designed these as posters to initiate discussion). We found that, because these stereotypes are so 'normalised', it was useful to examine them in conjunction with contrasting positive images. So we brought in a selection of children's books, some of which showed various stereotypes including gender, and some which presented alternative images. Our discussion led to the boys making their own 'non-stereotyped' children's books and toys.

A rather different 'course' on which one of us worked was a half-term project on developing work in single-sex groups in a junior school. This school (like many mixed schools attempting single-sex work) had a severe imbalance of girls and boys, with boys outnumbering girls by about $2\frac{1}{2}$:1. The aims of this project were to:

1 give both girls and boys the experience of working in a single sex group;
2 give girls increased access/opportunity to certain non-stereotypical activities and teacher time;
3 encourage greater assertiveness in the girls;
4 give boys the opportunity to reflect upon and share their feelings with other boys and, at the same time, to develop listening and discussion skills; and
5 encourage boys to examine the expectations stereotypically put upon boys and the influence this has on their behaviour towards girls, and to offer alternatives to these.

In addition it was hoped to:

1 enable the mixed groups to operate more collaboratively and fairly;
2 encourage teachers to examine their own attitudes which might reinforce stereotypes; and
3 formulate some future strategies for these particular groups, teachers and the school as a whole that challenge sexist behaviour, opportunities and expectations.

This work was carried out with two first-year junior classes with children aged seven and eight, their two female class teachers and the male Head teacher. The boys in both classes doubled up to work with the Head and one class teacher, while the other class teacher took all the girls. The work took place over six afternoon sessions.

The original idea for carrying out the work arose from concern over the way in which the boys dominated the classroom and the playground, and the amount of aggression among them (this seems to be one of the major concerns behind similar work in secondary schools). It was therefore decided that the work with the boys should focus particularly on the ways boys relate to one another. In describing this work we concentrate primarily on the work with the boys because of the emphasis in this book.[1]

It was decided to try focusing on 'active tutorial' work with

Figure 1

WHY DON'T MOST CHILDREN'S BOOKS Tell Us We Can Act Like This?

John tells his friend he is sad.

Mia likes to hammer and saw.

Luke likes to learn to sew.

Susie likes to go running.

Lets End STEREOTYPES in Children's Books!

Figure 2

the boys (although there are certain problems with this kind of work and we are far from uncritical of it[2]). The rationale behind active tutorial work or developmental work in tutor groups emphasises the development of such elements as supportive atmosphere, trust within the tutorial group, communication skills, the ability to project consequences for one's actions, and decision-making skills. The boys were brought together to sit in a circle in the hall and told that it had been decided to try some work on friendship and relating to one another. Each week they followed the same lesson structure. This was:

1 *An introductory activity* in the circle. For example, we played name games or clapping games.
2 *Discussion in pairs*. Each week we introduced this by an example from the teachers. The subject for discussion was kept very simple — 'Things that frighten me', 'Things I like about school'.
3 *Discussion in fours*. Each person related to the group what their partner had said in the pair discussion.
4 *Task*. Staying in small groups, the pupils carried out a task and shared the results: for example, putting some photographs in order to 'tell a story', writing a group collaborative poem.
5 *Physical activity*. This was an exercise to develop closeness between the boys, for example, 'trust walk', rocking one another.

The six-week project revealed some interesting issues. Each week at the beginning of the session the boys were restless, obviously felt unsure of what was happening and rather tense. They said things like: 'This is boring. Why can't we play with the computer toys?' They found the work difficult, but each week at the end (and progressively more so during the six weeks) they were clearly relaxed and enjoying themselves — sitting leaning against one another and the teachers in a relaxed atmosphere.

We felt that the plan to stick with the same lesson outline each week was crucial so that the boys began to understand what to expect. The intention of sticking to the same plan wavered after the first couple of weeks. However it was decided, because this was obviously something the boys found difficult, that we must give them more practice. This simple realisation was quite important — because at the beginning of lessons things didn't go as well as we'd hoped, we were tempted to abandon our plan. But giving the boys practice did pay off.

After six weeks, we felt that the boys were talking much more openly and listening much more carefully to one another. The Head and class teacher also felt that this *did* affect relationships positively back in the mixed class.

Although there seemed to be some positive feedback and this type of work may be a very useful starting point, we feel that it has its limitations. We do not feel that it can *fundamentally* affect the relationships between boys and girls.

Comments on specific anti-sexist courses

We believe that explicit anti-sexist courses such as we have been describing should not be offered as a solution to fundamental problems within the education system as a whole. In our view such courses as we have described are excellent and have a great deal to offer pupils, but they can only 'work' in a limited way because of the particular realities of the situation they were set up to combat. These 'structural' realities do not disappear by working with the pupils.

A course on anti-sexism puts the onus for change on the pupils. However, their behaviour is, in part at least, an outcome of the structure they operate within. This was particularly striking on one course we taught in a secondary school. During the initial few weeks of the course, taught to every first-year class (eight classes), almost every boy joined in the discussions enthusiastically, openly and with a great deal of empathy for other class members. However, over the following few weeks the boys began to be much less communicative about themselves; they became guarded; bullying seemed to be in evidence; and they began to question the validity of the work. Discussion became more difficult, and sometimes had to be abandoned in favour of more concrete activities. However, those classes whose teachers in other subjects were working in similar ways (for example, allowing for negotiation between teacher and pupil and including discussion work) continued to be able to discuss issues sensitively and with a great deal of obvious interest and involvement.

The whole school 'ethos' is vital in consideration of what

kinds of classroom method and teaching style can be implemented. In a school where the majority of classes are very formal, where the pupils are mainly passive learners, and where teaching methods are didactic and discussion kept to a minimum, it will be more difficult to teach in more informal ways. Pupil expectations of teacher roles may also be more rigidly stylised in keeping with the norms in the school. Additionally, teachers can find themselves in a dilemma when doing this kind of work. As one teacher said: 'It's difficult to get the balance right in this kind of work as far as pupil–teacher relationships are concerned. There's a thin line between being matey and sitting down chatting and being authoritarian'. The teacher wanting to create an atmosphere in which discussion can take place needs to develop a relationship with the pupils based on mutual regard and respect rather than authoritarian power. In many ways a classroom style which demands almost complete silence and obedience from pupils can be easier to attempt because the rules are much simpler. Moreover, the kind of relationship necessary for anti-sexist work with boys is extremely difficult to establish if there is only limited contact time, as is the case with many specific anti-sexist courses.

Another point which we found to be crucial concerns the way in which the needs for the course have been identified. While an anti-sexist focus may be helpful in identifying useful strategies and finding out what works well, we have realised that this has to be done in the broader context of looking at race and class oppression.

In secondary school, issues of equality of opportunity permeate every area of the curriculum; given this, they cannot be properly tackled as part of a separate course. Indeed, we found that this could be quite dangerous if it gives the illusion that they need not be tackled in other areas of school life. There are a great many important issues (for example, teacher expectations, teachers as role models) which have to be addressed if anti-sexist work is to be meaningful. If these are not taken into account across the curriculum, it is possible that the meanings and messages of an 'anti-sexist' course will be undermined or contradicted in other areas of the curriculum.

The advantage of 'a course' is that it will probably be taught by committed and enthusiastic teachers — if it is seen to be successful by other members of staff it may have a 'knock-on' effect within the school. This is particularly true where there is a policy of team teaching or an 'open door' policy where other members of staff are very actively encouraged to observe or join in lessons where possible. In this way we have seen some courses act as a spur to the development of a whole school approach to a policy within the curriculum.

Units of 'anti-sexist' work within the curriculum generally

Most teachers are either not in a position to or do not think it is desirable to set up a separate course in which to address issues of sexism. We have done 'support teaching' with many teachers in boys' schools to develop units of work which might be used elsewhere: for example, within English, humanities, home economics, social education, art or pastoral courses. All the materials which we produced are aimed at boys at top junior or lower secondary school levels (that is, ages nine to thirteen). Although some of the units could be suitable for girls as well as boys, they were specifically developed with boys in mind. If they were to be used with girls in mixed classrooms it would be necessary to rethink the context within which they are presented. As we have already stressed, certain styles and teaching methods are helpful in facilitating discussion of issues: method and style can be itself implicitly anti-sexist by challenging the stereotypes about how boys/men and women teachers should behave. For example, various teachers have become aware of themselves as 'role' models in terms of challenging sexist assumptions. Several men teachers talked to us about the dilemma of trying to get the boys to question male stereotypes of power and strength, on the one hand, yet found themselves relating to the boys in those terms on the other.

Didactic teaching methods seem to us inappropriate. So also do methods which try to lead the boys to a 'right' answer. We found, for example, that if we asked questions which sounded as though there was a 'right' answer, this inhibited real exploration. Where we asked for the pupil's own experience and gave ours, this seemed to generate a more lively and genuine discussion. It also enabled pupils to relate the issues

BRAVE MEN on television and in films are *Tough* and *Hard* BUT How Would They Get On In Real Life?

Would the Things They Do Be **BRAVE** OR **STUPID?**

Muck Tray Chocolates

† What would you think of someone who—
→ Was always looking for a fight?
→ Was never scared or sad?
→ Was always trying to impress people by acting tough?

CAROL ROSS

Worksheet A

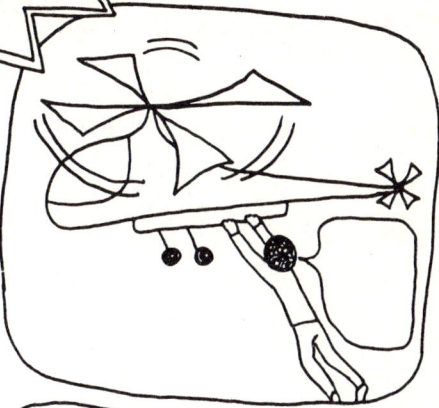

Worksheet B

more directly to themselves. Because of the nature of anti-sexist work, where children are being asked to reappraise the 'norms' of the world around them, it is important that scope is given for them to internalise the issues and relate them to their own experiences. If we are encouraging boys to explore their own experiences, it now seems to us vital that this includes space for them to reappraise the norms of a variety of circumstances surrounding their lives.

The remainder of this section gives examples of some of the anti-sexist units we have developed for use with boys. One unit of work was called 'Heroes and Stereotypes'. We wanted the boys to examine and question stereotypes of masculinity; reappraise a value system which prizes physical strength and aggression in males above all else; explore what we mean by the concept of a 'hero'; look critically at the images of masculinity presented by television, books, comics, magazines and cinema; and offer alternative images of masculinity.

When we used these materials some issues repeatedly arose. The central one was the problem of how to encourage pupils to re-evaluate the stereotypes involved in the concept of a 'hero', without either reinforcing those stereotypes or directly attacking pupils' sub-culture and, therefore, pupils themselves. We found that one way round this was to introduce humour into the materials as a way of involving the boys in their own gentle mockery of the concept of the television 'hero'. For example, the poster 'Brave Men' (Worksheet A) was used as a follow-on from some project work investigating various aspects of the television hero — for instance, violent images of men, and effects of violence on small children. This poster was intended to ask questions about how and why action is interpreted as brave or stupid. We found it useful also in moving the discussion from the subject of heroes to the question of bravery. The poster also stimulated discussion about different contexts in which the same action could be considered either brave or stupid. 'Ridiculous Heroes' (Worksheet B) was similarly used as a way of introducing humour.

Some teachers working on this topic felt initially that their approach led to resistance in the pupils. They felt that this was because they were trying to steer pupils to reach certain conclusions without being open about it. We found it more successful when we introduced the topic of 'heroes' with a clear hypothesis. For example: 'Television heroes encourage violence in young children'. The class then investigated this hypothesis.

Some teachers found that the point got muddled when they tried to develop the idea of an alternative 'hero'. They found it was better to talk about the concept of 'bravery'. We found it impossible to develop discussion in a non-stereotyped way because implicit in the concept of a 'hero' are qualities such as superior strength, intellect or skills. Furthermore, heroes are constantly superior rather than simply rising to the occasion.

Another 'unit' of work we have developed is called 'Talking Personally'. This was an attempt to provide materials aimed at challenging stereotypes of tough and competitive behaviour as 'masculine' and 'caring and gentle' behaviour as 'feminine'; attacking the idea that certain emotions are not 'masculine'; and helping the boys to express their more vulnerable feelings; and promoting understanding and trust within the group.

Materials in this unit included posters, role-play situations, poems, stories and photographs. For example, the poster 'I feel I'm 4 different people' (Worksheet C) was intended to explore how people get trapped in certain roles and images. It raises the different ways people experience themselves often in relation to the expectations others have of them. It was found to follow on well from bullying and was used to lead into gender stereotypes. All the materials in the units were produced with the intention of giving teachers something to trigger ideas. The materials were certainly never envisaged as perfected, finished products — many teachers have adapted them to suit their own situations. Worksheet C, for example, was used by one teacher in the following ways. In small groups the boys discussed what they thought was happening in the poster — how the boy was behaving in each picture. The teacher then gave some examples of different roles she took in her life, both now and as a child, for example 'When I'm a teacher I'm like this ... As a parent I'm like this ...'. The boys then made their own list of the roles they took in their lives (pupil, friend, Saturday job, brother, and so on). They talked and wrote about the way they behave in each role. This was followed by discussion about how they thought other people saw them in each role and expected them to behave. The discussion continued by focusing on which roles individual

Worksheet C

boys liked themselves most and least in. The boys discussed whether people find it hard to change the way they behave in each role — did people expect them to behave in certain ways? Some groups developed role play based on the ideas in the poster.

A second example from this unit was a prioritising exercise called 'How do boys feel in school?' (Worksheet D) which was used with small groups of boys as a starting point for discussing their experiences as first-year pupils in a large boys' inner-city comprehensive school. We found that this usually promoted a great deal of discussion and exchange of ideas which again was useful in breaking down some of the stereotypes of masculinity.

Comments on units of anti-sexist work within the curriculum generally

There are problems in attempting work on gender within existing curriculum areas. Much of the work we have been involved in has been concerned with developing an understanding of how 'stereotypes' operate, and why they are 'untrue'. We have found that introducing the concept of stereotypes is itself problematic. As we noted in relation to 'Heroes', lessons on stereotypes can actually reinforce stereotypes among some children. This can happen because of the apparent 'normality' of the stereotypes discussed. Thus, pointing out to pupils that stereotypes exist does not necessarily make them problematic for the children and encourage them to question them. We once observed a teacher who by pointing out stereotypes led the children to believe he was giving his own opinion about groups of people.

Another aspect of the problem is that so many stereotypes are offensive and emotive. In our experience, for some children to recognise a stereotype as destructive rather than as a description of reality, requires that the pupils have already gained the framework to understand it as such. We have tried to deal with this by discussing innocuous or silly statements — such as 'all children love baked beans', 'all boys are good at football', 'all teachers are unfair' — and ask pupils to talk about how people could get the idea that these statements were always true. We talked about images of children at school, on television, exaggerated stories from friends and advertisements. This led to

Boys Don't Cry

Worksheet D

How Do Boys Feel In School?

Boys behave differently when there are no girls around.	Teachers don't care what boys feel.
Most of the time at school, boys have to hide what they really feel.	It's harder to make real friends in secondary school than in primary school.
Being at an all-boys' school makes boys act more tough than they'd like to.	

1 Separate the cards into two piles: Agree and Disagree.
2 If there is more than 1 card in the Agree pile, put them in order from the one you most strongly agree with to the one you least strongly agree with.
3 If there is more than 1 card in the Disagree pile, put them in order from the one you most strongly disagree with to the one you least strongly disagree with.
4 Compare your piles with the people you're sitting next to.
5 Explain why you decided to put your cards in this order.
6 Think of some things *you* feel strongly about. Write them down as statements for discussion.

discourse about assumptions people make about others — because they are young or old; girls or boys; black or white.

Other issues include difficulty in identifying sexist patterns in society without directly criticising the boys themselves (or their families). Examining how sexism operates to oppress girls and women can be threatening and meaningless because it is difficult for boys to relate the issues directly to their lives and internalise them. 'Gender work is *against* boys — everyone's trying to tell me I'm wrong' is typical of the comments we have heard. In addition, the more explicit gender issues are difficult to discuss in a meaningful way because of the underlying relationships between boys themselves which we have described. As we have argued, there are pressures on boys in a boys' school to appear 'invulnerable', and until this dynamic is itself the object of discussion the outcome might be the creation of general unease, and perhaps more bullying.

These issues have led us to believe that anti-sexist work with boys must *start* with the boys' own interests, experiences and opinions. In Freire's (1972) terms, through re-thinking assumptions, actions may change:

> Students, as they are increasingly faced with problems relating to themselves in the world and with the world, will feel increasingly challenged and obliged to respond to that challenge. Because they apprehend the challenge as inter-related to other problems within a total context, not as a theoretical question, the resulting comprehension tends to be increasingly critical and thus constantly less alienated.

We have said throughout the book that we do not just view boys as 'the problem' in relation to sexism, but that institutional/ structural sexism also exists. We feel that any work done with pupils should be part of a process, therefore, which also challenges the values and assumptions on which the school as an institution is built.

Notes

1 The girls did some work with the computer, big tracks and robot (computer toys). They also carried out simple science experiments

around a theme (mechanics). Each week there was talk about what influence the presence of boys would have on their activity, and the ways they maintain their integrity and control in a mixed group. Both girls and class teacher said they looked forward to and enjoyed these sessions very much.

2 While the aims of active tutorial work are important, in our view they cannot be developed out of the context of the situations within which people live. Active tutorial type work may not take into account the social divisions within the group. Additionally, these aims need to be developed within all areas of the curriculum. We feel doubtful about whether they can be taught in one area of the curriculum and then 'internalised' and transferred to all other areas of school and life.

CHAPTER 6

In-Service Work
with Teachers

In this chapter we will outline some of the workshops which we have developed and tried out with teachers. All of these workshops were produced in response to requests from individual schools or teachers' centres and were used as a way of exploring some issues relating to sexism in the school structure and anti-sexist work with boys. We will also touch on some issues which arose in relation to them. We think that, just as children need to use active learning methods in order to develop skills in questioning, evaluating and coming to decisions, participatory methods are equally helpful for teachers' understanding. In our work with teachers we have, therefore, tried to develop materials and ways of working which encourage this. The materials are presented as they were actually used in workshops with teachers and may provide a useful basis for adaptation to the needs of both other school situations and other groups, for example, parents. We have selected a small number of workshops as illustrations of the kinds of materials developed. These do not provide a comprehensive coverage of all the issues relating to anti-sexist work in boys' schools or with boys, nor are they offered as 'models' of good practice — we merely hope they may 'spark off' ideas. When the materials were used with teachers, several points were considered, for example, what kind of need has been identified and by whom? who are the participants (within one department, whole school, women's group, equal opportunities working party, parents)? is the workshop a 'one-off' or part of a developing series? is it aimed at mixed groups of men and women, women only or men only? how many people are taking part? how much time is there for the workshop?

Workshops addressing sexism in the school structure

We have argued in this book that issues relating to inequality are not just curriculum issues and need to be addressed by the whole staff with regard to both the curriculum and the school organisation and structure. We began our anti-sexist work with a focus on working with teachers to develop curricular initiatives. However, we became increasingly aware of the need to put curricular development into a broader school context. Many teachers we have worked with expressed a wish to find a way to raise consciousness in their school and gain support for curricular work from colleagues. Many of the teachers felt that their schools needed to confront the way that sexism is institutionalised in the basic school structure. They felt that anti-sexist curricular initiatives alone put all the onus for change on the boys and resulted in a one-dimensional approach to equal opportunity work in school.

Prioritising exercises

We have often been asked to work with the Equal Opportunities Working Party in a particular school. In some boys' schools this kind of working party exists alongside the Women's Group. In other schools, the Women's Group has developed into a mixed working party to promote equal opportunities. One of the difficulties at the outset of the formation of a Working Party (as with the Women's Group) may be identifying where best to put energies in a situation where so much needs to be done. We have found it a useful exercise to sort and prioritise tasks: for example, members of the Working Party ranking their priorities according to statements on cards (Worksheet E) (some cards can be left blank so that participants add their own — if they wish they can also be asked to change the wording). This task is followed by comparing, in small groups, individual priorities and attempting to reach a consensus on which priorities it is most feasible to act on.

Worksheet E

Identifying possible action and prioritising tasks in a boys' school	
Look at bias in materials and investigate alternatives (start small).	Choose an area of the curriculum where a small initiative could be made: develop and monitor it.
Investigate harassment in the school and make recommendations for dealing with it.	Look at how bullying and violence operate within the school and make recommendations for dealing with it.
Act as a consciousness-raising group.	Initiate in-service work with colleagues.
Act as a support group, e.g. for teachers who may have been harassed or for teachers trying to promote curricular initiatives.	Look at how the structure and organisation of the school may contribute to inequality and oppression.
Examine ways in which a separate focus on sexism, racism and classism could be contributing to work in each area being less effective and develop strategies for changing the situation.	Produce a school policy.
Look at ways of informing and involving parents.	Please write your own.

Some of the boys' schools in which we have worked have begun by developing a whole school policy. We ourselves have mixed views about this. On the one hand, we feel that a policy is useful in that it acts as a reference point for future action and behaviour, and legitimises work in this area. In theory, the whole school is then committed to the implementation of the policy: if something is out of line with the policy it is possible to refer to it in support of change or challenge. It is a *starting point*, but no more than this. The policy itself is not a solution, but a programme for change. However, we have seen situations where the production of the policy is itself seen as an end. The ways in which the policy are implemented, monitored and adapted to meet the changing needs and situation of the school are all crucial.

Discussion 'openers'

We have attempted to explore some of the fundamental ways in which sexism is part of the school structure. Looking back, we feel that starting by trying to involve all staff in these discussions can be pretty disastrous. For example, one of us was asked to 'talk' to a large staff group about anti-sexist work in boys' schools. The school was closed early for this purpose. However, the group was much too large to develop any real discussion, and there were several members of staff who clearly did not want to be there. We now feel it is much better to start on a small scale, with a few committed and interested people who can slowly make progress towards involving others. We have often been told by frustrated teachers who feel isolated in the school that there are 'so many teachers who just don't feel it's important, or who make fun of, or sabotage attempts to tackle inequalities'.

Teachers who are alone in feeling that change needs to be made need support and the chance to discover that their experiences are shared by others. We have run several courses and weekend workshops which have aimed to enable teachers in boys' schools to share their experiences of how sexism operates within their institutions. One useful starting point for discussion is to use quotes from former discussions as 'openers' (see, for example, Worksheet F).

The quotes used in this worksheet are from teachers discussing sexism in boys' schools. They touch on teaching styles: discipline; bullying; pastoral care; staff meetings; school hierarchy; sexual harassment; competition.

Worksheet F

1 *Individually.* Pick out about three cards which you feel express something about which you feel strongly.
2 *In small groups.* Compare and discuss why you have chosen these cards. Write your own statements if you feel strongly about some aspect of sexism not expressed by any of the statements.
3 *In whole group.* Feedback from the small groups of most important points made in discussions.
4 Start thinking about strategies for action. You may like to follow this up by writing some kind of statement/s from the group.

'I feel a dilemma about my teaching — if I try to teach in a non-authoritarian way I am stereotyped as a soft teacher. But if I try to be more authoritarian I feel I am both reinforcing a system I hate and undermining other ways of working'.	'I feel that bullying among the boys is an acting out of the power structures of the school itself. I think it's too simple to say it's the fault of individual boys'.
'I think it's important when we are looking at sexism in school to see it as part of a more fundamental oppression affecting black, gay and working-class children'.	'Discipline is the responsibility of the Head of House. Kids who misbehave are taken off to see him. There is little consultation with the form tutor and never any negotiation between the boy involved, the form tutor and the class'.
'Our staff meetings reflect the hierarchical organisation of the school. They are didactic and many people feel too intimidated to give their opinions'.	'It's not that sexual harassment isn't taken seriously in my school, it's that it's not even recognised when it happens. There's no policy structure for dealing with it'.

'Not many women are a part of the hierarchy in my school, and if they are it's in the subjects people feel are 'female' like languages, English or special needs'.	'When I first started teaching in a boys' school I felt completely deskilled like a probationary teacher all over again. I felt incompetent. But now I think that a lot of what I felt to be my being ineffectual is a direct result of in-built sexism in the structure. I think this exists in a mixed school, too, of course, but exaggerated vastly in all boys' schools'.
Please write your own	

Sexism exercise

Another approach which we have found helpful involves looking at how we internalise sexist assumptions and stereotypes and, in turn, how these affect our attitudes towards men and women teachers and the boys we teach. An extension of this involves looking at the similarities between assumptions about women and those about other oppressed groups. For example, we might begin by asking the course participants to 'brainstorm' their responses to the word 'sexism'. From this, we ask people to work in small groups to develop a definition of sexism. We then ask the group to pick a statement. These statements vary depending on the situation we are working in, but might be something like this:

1 It is absolutely natural for boys to behave in aggressive, 'macho' ways and for girls to be quiet and passive. Men and women are supposed to complement one another and we should not try to change that fact. It is all down to our genes!
2 If women teachers have trouble with discipline in boys' schools that is their problem. They should leave.
3 Women teachers who are harassed bring it on themselves. They should dress and behave differently.

4   Sexism isn't an issue in a boys-only school. It's important only in work with girls — after all they're the ones whose education will be affected if boys muck around in the lessons.
5   Sexism operates within all social institutions and affects all those working within them. As such, the education system ought to ensure that its effects are reduced to a minimum wherever possible.
6   Don't misunderstand me. I'm against sexism like the next person. But I think discussion about sexism in school takes time away from the really important thing — and that's getting kids through the exams, isn't it?

The groups are asked to discuss the statement in relation to the following questions:

1   What are the values and assumptions implicit in the statement?
2   What kinds of power relations are at work here?
3   What are the implications for practice?

Practice situations

In our own experience it is much easier to run workshops and courses at schools and centres other than those in which we have been permanently working. Teachers on these courses have talked of their own lack of confidence in setting up workshops in their own school situations for colleagues. We feel that this relates to how authority and status are conferred in schools; unless we hold a high-status post it can be very hard to be recognised as having particular skills to offer in the school. Many teachers found it helpful to work in small groups on a 'practice' situation. For example, at one weekend conference, the participants divided into four groups of about six people. The groups were given a task — in each case two of the groups had the same task. These tasks were to devise a workshop on one of the following themes:

1   Boys' behaviour in the classroom.
2   Possible aims for anti-sexist work with boys.

Each group spent a session planning the workshop, for example, deciding how it should be organised and who should lead it. Two groups which had worked on different themes were then 'paired up' and ran their workshops for each other. At the end of each session the groups gave one another feedback on the workshop. A third session allowed each group independently to assess how well their work had gone, how it might be changed or adapted, and whether it would be a suitable session to organise in school. This was one way in which we felt that some new and exciting ways of organising discussion and action were being generated in a 'safe' environment and, at the same time, there was an increased understanding of the issues involved for those involved in the 'practice'. An example of how this can work in school is that of a women's group in a boys' school taking on the planning and running of a staff conference. In this particular case, the number of staff was fairly small (under 50) and the women divided into small groups of three or four to work together on planning and running workshops with different themes — they practised these workshops on each other before running the sessions with other staff. Where these kinds of initiative have been taken they have generated a sense of excitement because they allow everyone to participate directly in bringing about change at a structural level.

Exploring issues in anti-sexist work with boys

We have run many workshops aimed at exploring strategies for working with boys and some issues involved in such work. One way in which we have found it helpful to start discussion about this work is by using a questionnaire, such as Worksheet G. This is filled in by workshop participants individually and then can be discussed in pairs — looking particularly at statements over which people disagree and exploring why this disagreement occurs. This exercise can be used as a very general 'way in' to some of the issues and can be followed by a focus on any one of the statements in ensuing workshops.

Worksheet G

	Agree	Disagree	Don't know
The only way we can do useful anti-sexist work with boys is within an overall school policy which seeks to change the structure and organisation of the school.			
Anti-sexist work cannot be just a part of one course — it must be part of a general change in the curriculum.			
Teachers are role models for children and therefore it is essential that they look at their own sexist attitudes and assumptions first before trying to change their pupils.			
Boys are not the 'problem' in relation to sexism. Their behaviour is a reflection of the way in which masculinity is constructed in this society.			
Anti-sexist work with boys must be done as part of a wider examination of inequality generally.			
Anti-sexist work with boys should be concerned with 'what's in it for them' rather than with just challenging their sexism.			

Aims of anti-sexist work with boys

We have found considerable disagreement over what the aims of anti-sexist work with boys might be. As a way of reaching some consensus we produced a list of possible aims which can be practised as a 'diamond nine' exercise (see Worksheet H). In this exercise participants, working in pairs, arrange the statements in a 'diamond' shape (the cards can be added to and altered as required). When the cards are prioritised small groups of people compare their priorities, trying to reach a consensus and discussing ways in which the aims can be put into practice.

Worksheet H

To teach boys home economics and child care (how to look after children).	To help boys communicate on a more personal level.
To help boys empathise with other people.	To help boys understand that there are ways of behaving other than 'macho'.
To promote collaborative rather than competitive work.	To gain an understanding of how oppression and exploitation operate.
To explore with boys ways in which people are sex-role stereotyped.	To look at sexist images in the media and in books.
To help boys learn to take responsibility for other people.	To help boys listen to other people.
Please write your own.	

Problems and issues in addressing sexism with boys

As we suggested in Chapter 5, various problems have emerged in attempting anti-sexist work with boys. Several teachers have talked about experiencing similar problems and we have found it helpful to share these experiences as a way of working towards finding solutions. We have also developed workshops with teachers who are just starting anti-sexist work with boys which aim to anticipate and, hopefully, avoid some of the 'pitfalls'. Where this is attempted quotations such as those from teachers on Worksheet I can be used. These may be considered in relation to anti-sexist curricular initiatives being taken within particular schools, with a focus on those which seem particularly relevant. We feel it is important for workshops to end on a positive note rather than focus only on 'problems'! With this in mind, a workshop focusing on problems can include time being given to a compilation of strategies for overcoming them.

Worksheet I

'Lots of classroom practice in boys' schools can be implicitly non-sexist such as presenting a balanced curriculum, providing resources which reflect women's achievements as well as men. When explicit anti-sexist work is being attempted this must determine the content of the lesson and include looking at the power structures and oppression involved. It must also occur within a context which recognises that the victims of sexism are girls and women although boys and men are also affected by it'.

'Presenting work which directly deals with exploring stereotypes is extremely difficult. It is easy to end up reinforcing stereotyped norms. Pointing out a stereotype doesn't necessarily make it problematic. It isn't self-evident that stereotypes are damaging unless you are already looking at them from a particular position'.

'It can be difficult to identify things as sexist in society without putting the kids down for how they live or what they like. For example, domestic roles at home; macho 'heroes' in comic books or on television'.

'Equal opportunities work with boys isn't necessarily anti-sexist. It doesn't necessarily challenge sex roles and assumptions. For example, some boys doing cooking said it would be useful "in case my wife is in hospital".'

'The dynamics of the classroom can undermine the anti-sexist content of the lesson. For example, the way the boys relate to a woman teacher; the way the boys relate to each other; the way a woman and a man teacher teaching relate to each other and the boys, e.g. who takes charge of discipline'.

'Focusing on sexism in isolation from other forms of oppression can inadvertently be racist or classist'.

'It's difficult to make issues of gender meaningful and related to the boys' lives, but if they are not able to internalise them, the anti-sexist work is meaningless'.

'Anti-sexist work with boys is in itself a contradiction. What do you say to boys in my class who said: "Gender work is *against* boys"? Particularly when the boys themselves are oppressed in so many other ways'.

Currently teachers in many schools are besieged with different demands and requirements from the education authority, from industry and from parents. They often have to prioritise issues which all seem equally important. Teachers are also under pressure from the media in relation to such things as discipline. It is not surprising, therefore, that many teachers in boys' schools do not see gender issues as an urgent priority. One important strategy for working in boys' schools is to show the ways in which anti-sexist work is good educational practice. Also anti-sexist strategies are often in line with recommendations made in other reports with a different focus. For example, any anti-sexist strategy stressing the importance of collaborative activities for boys would be in line with suggestions made about collaboration in reference to mixed ability teaching or the educational needs of bi-lingual pupils in the main-stream classroom. In this chapter we have looked briefly at some of the ways teachers can take on for themselves issues to do with examining sexism in school. It is important to recognise that there are limitations of the sorts of changes that can be made in schools without social change. We sometimes tend to look on schools as a vehicle for changing society. There may indeed be this potential but it is important at the same time to recognise them as perpetuating society. The next chapter briefly places schools as an institution within their broader social context.

CHAPTER 7

Conclusions

In this book we have focused on sexism in schools, primarily in boys' schools. We have addressed the issue of how boys relate to each other, to male and female teachers, to the position of women in the school, and to sexism in the curriculum, structure and organisation of the school.

We have tried to address the issue of sexism from two perspectives. These relate to approaches taken to exploring the issue more generally in wider society. One is concerned with looking at individual experiences of sexism and sexual inequalities, focusing on the socialisation of women and men, the dynamics between them, and on developing various personal strategies for change. The other is related to the political context, and involves examining sexism as a reflection of the socio-economic system, analysing social relations in terms of dominant power structures and institutions. We have tried throughout this book not only to describe various manifestations of sexism at an individual level, but to relate these to the power and value structures of the institution.

Schools are society in microcosm. Their purpose is to perpetuate the values and ideologies dominant in society, and they are organised so as to achieve this. These values and ideologies are those of the white, middle-class male. Boys learn to identify with the dominant group and its belief system which rewards achievement in competitive and individualistic, rather than collaborative, collective, terms. Success for one group means failure for another. This has clear implications for the socialisation and education of boys. We saw in earlier chapters how boys interrelate, approach their work, working in a more individualistic, competitive and aggressive way than did girls, and how the school system itself reinforces this, especially in boys-only schools.

We have argued that the most socially valued spheres are the domain of men. These are areas which relate to science and technology, the centre of economic and political power in our industrialised, technological society. We have also argued that women's roles exist essentially in relation to supporting and facilitating work done by men. According to Overfield (1982) 'the male (white, middle-class, heterosexual) is taken as the norm against which everything else is measured', and

> if the male, or masculine, is the baseline from which everything else is measured, anything else tends automatically to be defined as deviant, prohibited, or an expression of 'otherness' .... Conversely, it is seen as an achievement to *reach* male standards, to become *equal* on male terms, to attain accredited status.

She describes two fundamental results:

(1) Women are defined not on their own terms, not even from their own point of view, but in relation to the male — to men's wants, prejudices and fears;

(2) The male/female distinction is the first of a long line of divisions: masculine/feminine; subject/object; good/bad; logical/emotional — and the whole point of having categories means that entire populations are placed according to certain 'features'.

This has implications for the ways boys are socialised and develop. In Chapter 1 we looked at some socialising factors in the construction of masculinity, for instance, expectations of boys and the pressure on them to adopt masculine 'values' and behaviour. In our society any behaviour which falls outside of these 'norms' is 'unacceptable'. Thus in schools, and particularly in boys' schools, boys are at great pains to dissociate themselves from any traits regarded as female. We have discussed how this affects the ways they express themselves and relate to others.

Most of us generally accept what is called 'knowledge', especially 'scientific knowledge', as being unquestionable and unassailable 'truth'. Yet what is regarded as 'knowledge' is as socially constructed as is the use to which it is put. Western science has been developed within the tradition of 'objective' thought; the whole basis on which 'scientific truths' are established is supposed to be 'detached' and therefore beyond question. Furthermore, the discipline reflects 'male' qualities and these reinforce each other to promote an image of 'male rationality' which is supposed to be superior to any other form of consciousness. The whole notion of male rationality in this culture affects boys by teaching them to regard emotionality with suspicion and to avoid expressing their emotions (with the exception of anger) at all costs. It leads to the sorts of rigid and restricted way of boys interrelating which we describe in Chapters 1 and 2.

In our view, therefore, any meaningful anti-sexist work must involve changes in the curriculum which revise our concepts of knowledge and education. In Chapter 5 we talked about specific anti-sexist strategies with boys which could be used within the existing curriculum. This is, clearly, the area to which teachers have individual access with regard to implementing change. What types of change should be implemented is a contentious issue. It has been tempting to make those subjects which are not seen as 'boys' subjects more 'objective' and 'rational' in order to attract boys to them. For example, one recent approach to attracting more boys into Home Economics has been to try to reconstruct it as a more 'scientific' subject. This may attract boys initially but it does nothing to break down barriers between what is 'male' and what is 'female', what is 'affective' and what is 'objective'.

It is vital to understand the ways our social system is reflected and reproduced in our school system. We have suggested that, in society, the roles and 'characteristics' claimed by the dominant groups will determine the roles and 'characteristics' assigned to subordinate groups. It is therefore possible to learn a great deal about the position of subordinate groups through examining the dominant groups. In this book we look mainly at issues surrounding the education of boys because we believe this will help to illuminate prevailing structures in all educational systems. Within this, more explicitly, we believe that the ways boys are socialised and educated have direct implications for girls' education. In an important sense, 'masculinity' exists in direct contrast to femininity; what is 'feminine' is defined by what is 'masculine', and 'women's roles' are defined as complementary (and supportive) to 'men's roles'. We have looked at various 'male' attributes and examined the implications of how and what boys develop (or don't develop). Working with boys and coming to understand some of the ways they are socialised and educated has given us a clearer understanding about the position of girls.

Bibliography

Archer, J. (1979), *Animals under Stress*, Edward Arnold.

Archer, J. and Lloyd, B. (1982), *Sex and Gender*, Penguin Books, p. 105.

Archer, J. and Westerman, K. (1981), 'Sex differences in the aggressive behaviour of school children', *Brit. J. of Social and Clinical Psychology*.

Askew, S. and Ross, C. (1984), *Anti-sexist Work with Boys*, ILEA.

Assessment and Performance Unit (1983), *Language Performance in Schools*, Primary Survey Report No. 2, HMSO.

Baran, Graz (1986), 'Re-thinking the science curriculum', in *Secondary Issues: Some Approaches to Equal Opportunities in Secondary Schools*, ILEA.

Barrs, M. and Pidgeon, S. (1986), 'Gender and Reading', in *Language Matters*, ILEA, Centre for Language in Primary Education.

Bem, S.L. (1974), 'The measurement of psychological androgyny', *J. of Consulting and Clinical Psychology*, 42, pp. 155–62.

Benn, M. (1985), 'Isn't sexual harassment really about masculinity?', *Spare Rib*, 156, July.

Browne, N. and France, P. (1985), 'Only cissies wear dresses: a look at sexist talk in the nursery', in Gaby Weiner (ed.), *Just a Bunch of Girls*, Open University Press, p. 150.

Carabis, E. and Dodds, V. (1984), 'All in a day's work', unpublished paper, London University, p. 5.

Carricoates, K. (1978), 'Dinosaurs in the classroom: a re-examination of some aspects of the hidden curriculum in primary schools', *Women's Studies International Quarterly*, 1 (4), pp. 353–64.

Cockroft Report (1982), *Mathematics Counts: Report of the Committee of Inquiry into the Teaching of Mathematics in Schools*, HMSO.

Connell, B. (1985), 'A New Man', in *The English Curriculum*, ILEA, English Centre Publication.

Davis, J. and Tichner, J. (1986), 'Can girls build — or do they choose not to? A study of girls and boys using construction materials', in *Primary Teaching Studies*, Vol. No. 1, Polytechnic of North London.

Davison, J. (1985), 'Boys will be ...?', in *The English Curriculum: Gender*, ILEA, English Centre Publication.

Eggleston Report (1986), *Education for Some: The Educational and Vocational Experience of 15–18-year-old Members of Ethnic Minority Groups*, Trenthan Books.

EOC Report (1982), *What's in it for boys?*

Fish Report (1985), *Educational Opportunities for All*, ILEA.

Freire, P. (1972), *Pedagogy of the Oppressed*, Penguin.

French, J. (1986), 'Gender and the classroom', *New Society*, 7 March.

Fuller, M. (1980), 'Black girls in a London comprehensive school', in R. Deem (ed.), *Schooling for Women's Work*, Routledge and Kegan Paul.

Goldenberg, S. (1986), 'Race, sex and the missing link', *Teaching London Kids*, 23, p. 22.

Hargreaves, D. (1983), article in *New Society*, 10 March.

Hodson, P. (1984), *Men: an Investigation into the Emotional Male*, Ariel Books.

ILEA (1985), Report of the work of the working party on single sex and co-education, unpublished.

ILEA (1985), Junior survey. Referred to by Barrs, M and Pidgeon, S. (1986), in 'Gender and Reading', *Language Matters*. No. 1

Ingham, M (1984), *Men*, Century Publishing Company.

Kuhn, D., Nash, S.C. and Bruchan, L. (1978), 'Sex-role concepts of two- and three-year-olds', *Child Development*, 49, pp 445–51.

Levinson, D. (1978), *The Seasons of a Man's Life*, New York, Knopf.

Lloyd, T. (1985), *Working with Boys*, National Youth Bureau.

Lloyd, T. (1986), 'Boyswork: Discussion Paper No.1', unpublished.

Mahoney, P. (1985) *Schools for the Boys*, Hutchinson.

Metcalf, A. and Humphries, M. (1985), *The Sexuality of Men*, Pluto Press.

Minhas, R. (1986), 'Race, gender and class — making the connections', in *Secondary Issues: Some Approaches to Equal Opportunities in Secondary Schools*, ILEA.

Morrison, P. and Eardley, T. (1985), *About Men*, Channel 4 film.

Newson, J. and Newson, E. (1968), *Four Years Old in an Urban Community*, London, Allen and Unwin.

Newson, J. and Newson, E. (1984), 'Parents' perspectives on children's behaviour at school', in N. Frude and H. Gault (eds.), *'Disruptive Behaviour in Schools'*, John Wiley.

Nicholson, J. (1984), *Men and Women: How Different Are They?*, Oxford University Press.

O'Hagan, F.J. and Edmunds, G. (1982), 'Pupils' attitudes towards teachers: strategies for controlling disruptive behaviour', *Brit. J. of Ed. Psychology* 52 (3), November, pp. 331–40.

Olweus, D. (1978), *Aggression in the Schools: Bullies and Whipping Boys*, John Wiley.

Overfield, K. (1982), 'The packaging of women: science and our sexuality', in *On the Problems of Men,* eds. S. Friedman and E. Sarah, The Women's Press, pp. 67–70.

Riley, K. (1985), 'Black girls speak for themselves', in Gaby Weiner (ed.), *Just a Bunch of Girls,* Open University Press.

Rose, R.M., Gordon T.P. and Bernstein, I.S. (1972), 'Plasma testosterone levels in male rhesus monkeys: influences of sexual and social stimuli', *Science, 178,* pp. 643–5.

Sandra, M. (1982), 'A Study of the experience of girls and boys in the Secondary mixed ability classroom in one school'. M.A. dissertation, Institute of Education, University of London.

Sandra, M. (1985), 'Ruler Banging and Other Noises', in *The English Curriculum: Gender,* ILEA, English Centre Publication.

Seidler, V. (1980), 'Raging Bull', in *Achilles' Heel,* No. 5, p. 9.

Smith, P.K. and Green, M. (1975), 'Aggressive behaviour in English nurseries and playgroups: sex differences and responses to adults', *Child Development, 46,* pp. 211–14.

Smith, C. and Lloyd, B.B. (1978), 'Maternal behaviour and perceived sex of infant', *Child Development, 49,* pp. 1263–5.

Spender, Dale (1982), *Invisible Women,* Writers and Readers, London.

Stanworth, M. (1981), *Gender and Schooling,* Hutchinson.

Suleiman, L. and Suleiman, S. (1985), 'An education in racism and sexism', in Gaby Weiner (ed.), *Just a Bunch of Girls,* Open University Press.

Tingle, S. (1985), 'Going mixed', in *The English Curriculum: Gender,* ILEA, English Centre Publication.

Tolson, A. (1977), *The Limits of Masculinity,* Tavistock.

Toynbee, P. (1985), 'So many bright little girls — and so many humble young women', in *The English Curriculum: Gender,* ILEA, English Centre Publication.

Walden, R. and Walkerdine, V. (1982), *Girls and Mathematics: The Early Years,* Bedford Way Papers, No. 8, University of London, Institute of Education.

Walden, R. and Walkerdine, V. (1985), *Girls and Mathematics: From Primary to Secondary Schooling,* Bedford Way Papers, No. 24, University of London, Institute of Education.

Walker, S. and Barton, L. (1983), *Gender, Class and Education,* The Falmer Press, p. 3.

Walkerdine, V. (1981), 'Sex, power and pedagogy', in *Science Education, 38,* Spring.

Weiner, G. (ed.), *Just a Bunch of Girls,* Open University Press.

Whitehead, F. *et al.* (1977) Children and their books', in *Schools Council Research Studies,* Macmillan Education.

Index